to

_____

from

_____

FAMILY
CHRISTIAN
PRESS

table of contents

God's Promises About . . .

INTRODUCTION

God has made plenty of promises to you—extreme promises—and He intends to keep every single one of them. To make things understandable, God bundled everything up in a single book. That book, of course, is the Holy Bible.

This text contains Bible verses that spell out God's promises concerning a wide range of topics. But wait, there's more! Each chapter also contains some thought-provoking ideas from notable Christian thinkers.

So the next time you find yourself pondering God's promises, ponder no more. Instead of scratching your head, pick up your Bible . . . and start reading. When you do, you'll be reminded that you're extremely loved and extremely blessed . . . now and forever.

God's Promises About...
ABUNDANCE

The master was full of praise. "Well done, my good and faithful servant. You have been faithful in handling this small amount, so now I will give you many more responsibilities. Let's celebrate together!"

Matthew 25:21 NLT

**I am come that they might have life,
and that they might have it more abundantly.**

John 10:10 KJV

If you give, you will receive. Your gift will return to you in full measure, pressed down, shaken together to make room for more, and running over. Whatever measure you use in giving—large or small—it will be used to measure what is given back to you.

Luke 6:38 NLT

Now this I say, he who sows sparingly will also reap sparingly, and he who sows bountifully will also reap bountifully.

2 Corinthians 9:6 NASB

more words of wisdom

The only way you can experience abundant life is to surrender your plans to Him.

Charles Stanley

The gift of God is eternal life, spiritual life, abundant life through faith in Jesus Christ, the Living Word of God.

Anne Graham Lotz

God's riches are beyond anything we could ask or even dare to imagine! If my life gets gooey and stale, I have no excuse.

Barbara Johnson

Jesus intended for us to be overwhelmed by the blessings of regular days. He said it was the reason he had come: "I am come that they might have life, and that they might have it more abundantly."

Gloria Gaither

-A Tip-

God will provide for your needs if you stay focused on doing His will.

God's Promises About...
ACCEPTING CHRIST

**For the wages of sin is death, but the gift of God
is eternal life in Christ Jesus our Lord.**

Romans 6:23 HCSB

*For God so loved the world that He gave His only begotten
Son, that whoever believes in Him should not perish but have
everlasting life.*

John 3:16 NKJV

*Truly, truly, I say to you, he who hears My word, and believes
Him who sent Me, has eternal life, and does not come into
judgment, but has passed out of death into life. Truly, truly, I
say to you, an hour is coming and now is, when the dead will
hear the voice of the Son of God, and those who hear will
live.*

John 5:24-25 NASB

*The Spirit of God, who raised Jesus from the dead, lives in
you. And just as he raised Christ from the dead, he will give
life to your mortal body by this same Spirit living within you.*

Romans 8:11 NLT

*We know very well that we are not set right with God by rule-
keeping but only through personal faith in Jesus Christ.*

Galatians 2:16 MSG

more words of wisdom

The amount of power you experience to live a victorious, triumphant Christian life is directly proportional to the freedom you give the Spirit to be Lord of your life!

Anne Graham Lotz

Choose Jesus Christ! Deny yourself, take up the Cross, and follow Him—for the world must be shown. The world must see, in us, a discernible, visible, startling difference.

Elisabeth Elliot

The most profound essence of my nature is that I am capable of receiving God.

St. Augustine

A man can accept what Christ has done without knowing how it works; indeed, he certainly won't know how it works until he's accepted it.

C. S. Lewis

-A Tip-

It is critically important to be certain that you have welcomed Christ into your heart. If you've accepted Christ, congratulations. If not, the time to accept Him is now!

promises for life

God's Promises About...
ASKING HIM

So I say to you, ask, and it will be given to you; seek, and you will find; knock, and it will be opened to you. For everyone who asks receives, and he who seeks finds, and to him who knocks it will be opened.

Luke 11:9-10 NKJV

From now on, whatever you request along the lines of who I am and what I am doing, I'll do it. That's how the Father will be seen for who he is in the Son. I mean it. Whatever you request in this way, I'll do.

John 14:13-14 MSG

You did not choose me, but I chose you and appointed you to go and bear fruit—fruit that will last. Then the Father will give you whatever you ask in my name.

John 15:16 NIV

Do not worry about anything, but pray and ask God for everything you need, always giving thanks.

Philippians 4:6 NCV

You do not have, because you do not ask God.

James 4:2 NIV

EXTREME

more words of wisdom

When will we realize that we're not troubling God with our questions and concerns? His heart is open to hear us—his touch nearer than our next thought—as if no one in the world existed but us. Our very personal God wants to hear from us personally.

Gigi Graham Tchividjian

All we have to do is to acknowledge our need, move from self-sufficiency to dependence, and ask God to become our hiding place.

Bill Hybels

Don't be afraid to ask your heavenly Father for anything you need. Indeed, nothing is too small for God's attention or too great for his power.

Dennis Swanberg

When you ask God to do something, don't ask timidly; put your whole heart into it.

Marie T. Freeman

-A Tip-

If you need something, ask. And remember this: God is listening, and He wants to hear from you right now.

promises for life

God's Promises About...
ATTITUDE

There is one thing I always do. Forgetting the past and straining toward what is ahead, I keep trying to reach the goal and get the prize for which God called me . . . .

Philippians 3:13-14 NCV

Come near to God, and God will come near to you. You sinners, clean sin out of your lives. You who are trying to follow God and the world at the same time, make your thinking pure.

James 4:8 NCV

Those who are pure in their thinking are happy, because they will be with God.

Matthew 5:8 NCV

**For God has not given us a spirit of fear,
but of power and of love and of a sound mind.**

2 Timothy 1:7 NLT

Keep your eyes focused on what is right, and look straight ahead to what is good.

Proverbs 4:25 NCV

EXTREME

more words of wisdom

I became aware of one very important concept I had missed before: my attitude—not my circumstances—was what was making me unhappy.

Vonette Bright

Attitude is more important than the past, than education, than money, than circumstances, than what people do or say. It is more important than appearance, giftedness, or skill.

Charles Swindoll

You've heard the saying, "Life is what you make it." That means we have a choice. We can choose to have a life full of frustration and fear, but we can just as easily choose one of joy and contentment.

Dennis Swanberg

Do you wonder where you can go for encouragement and motivation? Run to Jesus.

Max Lucado

-A Tip-

Learn about Jesus and His attitude. Then try and do what Jesus would do.

promises for life

God's Promises About...
BEHAVIOR

Don't be deceived: God is not mocked. For whatever a man sows he will also reap, because the one who sows to his flesh will reap corruption from the flesh, but the one who sows to the Spirit will reap eternal life from the Spirit.

Galatians 6:7-8 HCSB

Light shines on the godly, and joy on those who do right. May all who are godly be happy in the LORD and praise his holy name.

Psalm 97:11-12 NLT

Even a child is known by his actions,
by whether his conduct is pure and right.

Proverbs 20:11 NIV

Therefore, get your minds ready for action, being self-disciplined, and set your hope completely on the grace to be brought to you at the revelation of Jesus Christ. As obedient children, do not be conformed to the desires of your former ignorance but, as the One who called you is holy, you also are to be holy in all your conduct.

1 Peter 1:13-15 HCSB

Lead a tranquil and quiet life in all godliness and dignity.

1 Timothy 2:2 HCSB

more words of wisdom

We are to leave an impression on all those we meet that communicates whose we are and what kingdom we represent.

Lisa Bevere

Never support an experience which does not have God as its source and faith in God as its result.

Oswald Chambers

The best evidence of our having the truth is our walking in the truth.

Matthew Henry

I don't care what a man says he believes with his lips. I want to know with a vengeance what he says with his life and his actions.

Sam Jones

The temptation of the age is to look good without being good.

Brennan Manning

-A Tip-

If you're not sure that it's the right thing to do, don't do it! And if you're not sure that it's the truth, don't tell it.

promises for life

God's Promises About...
BIBLE

Blessed are those who hunger and thirst for righteousness, for they will be filled.

Matthew 5:6 NIV

Every word of God is pure: he is a shield unto them that put their trust in him.

Proverbs 30:5 KJV

For I am not ashamed of the gospel, because it is God's power for salvation to everyone who believes.

Romans 1:16 HCSB

For the word of God is quick, and powerful, and sharper than any two-edged sword, piercing even to the dividing asunder of soul and spirit, and of the joints and marrow, and is a discerner of the thoughts and intents of the heart.

Hebrews 4:12 KJV

Jesus answered and said unto him, If a man love me, he will keep my words: and my Father will love him, and we will come unto him, and make our abode with him.

John 14:23 KJV

more words of wisdom

I believe the Bible is the best gift God has ever given to men. All the good from the Savior of the world is communicated to us through this book.

Abraham Lincoln

I study the Bible as I gather apples. First, I shake the whole tree that the ripest might fall. Then I shake each limb; I shake each branch and every twig. Then, I look under every leaf.

Martin Luther

**The devil is not afraid
of a Bible that has dust on it.**

Anonymous

-A Tip-

The Bible is the best-selling book of all time . . . for good reason. Ruth Bell Graham, wife of evangelist Billy Graham, believes in the importance of God's Word: "The Reference Point for the Christian is the Bible. All values, judgments, and attitudes must be gauged in relationship to this Reference Point." Make certain that you're an avid reader of God's best-seller, and make sure that you keep reading it as long as you live!

GOd's Promises About...
CELEBRATION

At the dedication of the wall of Jerusalem, the Levites were sought out from where they lived and were brought to Jerusalem to celebrate joyfully the dedication with songs of thanksgiving and with the music of cymbals, harps and lyres.

Nehemiah 12:27 NIV

David and the whole house of Israel were celebrating with all their might before the LORD, with songs and with harps, lyres, tambourines, sistrums and cymbals.

2 Samuel 6:5 NIV

This is the day the LORD has made; we will rejoice and be glad in it.

Psalm 118:24 NKJV

Delight thyself also in the LORD; and he shall give thee the desires of thine heart.

Psalm 37:4 KJV

Shout for joy to the LORD, all the earth. Worship the LORD with gladness; come before him with joyful songs.

Psalm 100:1-2 NIV

EXTREME

more words of wisdom

**If you can forgive the person you were,
accept the person you are,
and believe in the person you will become,
you are headed for joy. So celebrate your life.**

Barbara Johnson

Joy is the direct result of having God's perspective on our daily lives and the effect of loving our Lord enough to obey His commands and trust His promises.

Bill Bright

He wants us to have a faith that does not complain while waiting, but rejoices because we know our times are in His hands—nail-scarred hands that labor for our highest good.

Kay Arthur

I know nothing, except what everyone knows—if there when God dances, I should dance.

W. H. Auden

-A Tip-

Today is a cause for celebration: Psalm 118:24 has clear instructions for the coming day: "This is the day which the LORD has made; let us rejoice and be glad in it." Plan your day—and your life—accordingly.

promises for life

God's Promises About...
CHANGE

There is a time for everything, and a season for every activity under heaven.

Ecclesiastes 3:1 NIV

John said, "Change your hearts and lives because the kingdom of heaven is near."

Matthew 3:2 NCV

I am the LORD, and I do not change.

Malachi 3:6 NLT

Therefore do not worry about tomorrow, for tomorrow will worry about itself. Each day has enough trouble of its own.

Matthew 6:34 NIV

The prudent see danger and take refuge, but the simple keep going and suffer from it.

Proverbs 27:12 NIV

EXTREME

more words of wisdom

The secret of contentment in the midst of change is found in having roots in the changeless Christ—the same yesterday, today and forever.

Ed Young

Conditions are always changing; therefore, I must not be dependent upon conditions. What matters supremely is my soul and my relationship to God.

Corrie ten Boom

When you're through changing, you're through!

John Maxwell

**With God, it isn't who you were that matters;
it's who you are becoming.**

Liz Curtis Higgs

-A Tip-

If a big change is called for . . . don't be afraid to make a big change—sometimes, one big leap is better than a thousand baby steps.

God's Promises About...
CHARACTER

The righteousness of the blameless clears his path, but the wicked person will fall because of his wickedness.

Proverbs 11:5 HCSB

Do not be deceived: "Evil company corrupts good habits."

1 Corinthians 15:33 NKJV

We also rejoice in our afflictions, because we know that affliction produces endurance, endurance produces proven character, and proven character produces hope.

Romans 5:3-4 HCSB

A good name is to be chosen over great wealth.

Proverbs 22:1 HCSB

**As the water reflects the face,
so the heart reflects the person.**

Proverbs 27:19 HCSB

EXTREME

more words of wisdom

Character cannot be developed in ease and quiet. Only through experience of trial and suffering can the soul be strengthened, vision cleared, ambition inspired, and success achieved.

Helen Keller

Right actions done for the wrong reason do not help to build the internal quality of character called a "virtue," and it is this quality or character that really matters.

C. S. Lewis

Character is what you are in the dark.

D. L. Moody

What lessons about honor did you learn from your childhood? Are you living what you learned today?

Dennis Swanberg

Let God use times of waiting to mold and shape your character. Let God use those times to purify your life and make you into a clean vessel for His service.

Henry Blackaby and Claude King

-A Tip-

Remember: Character is more important than popularity.

promises for life

God's Promises About...
CHARITY

In every way I've shown you that by laboring like this, it is necessary to help the weak and to keep in mind the words of the Lord Jesus, for He said, "It is more blessed to give than to receive."

Acts 20:35 HCSB

And above all things have fervent charity among yourselves: for charity shall cover the multitude of sins.

1 Peter 4:8 KJV

Instruct those who are rich in the present age not to be arrogant or to set their hope on the uncertainty of wealth, but on God, who richly provides us with all things to enjoy. Instruct them to do good, to be rich in good works, to be generous, willing to share.

1 Timothy 6:17-18 HCSB

And above all these things put on charity, which is the bond of perfectness.

Colossians 3:14 KJV

**Be generous: Invest in acts of charity.
Charity yields high returns.**

Ecclesiastes 11:1 MSG

more words of wisdom

What we give to the poor for Christ's sake is what we carry with us when we die.

Peter Marin

For many of us, the great obstacle to charity lies not in our luxurious living or desire for more money, but in our fear of insecurity.

C. S. Lewis

**Charity is the pure gold
which makes us rich in eternal wealth.**

Jean Pierre Camus

I never look at the masses as my responsibility. I look at the individual. I can love only one person at a time. I can feed only one person at a time. Just one, one, one. You get closer to Christ by coming closer to each other.

Mother Teresa

-A Tip-

Investing in God's work, including helping the poor, is always the right thing to do.

promises for life

God's Promises About...
CHEERFULNESS

A happy heart is like a continual feast.

Proverbs 15:15 NCV

**Jacob said, "For what a relief it is
to see your friendly smile.
It is like seeing the smile of God!"**

Genesis 33:10 NLT

A merry heart does good, like medicine.

Proverbs 17:22 NKJV

*Do everything readily and cheerfully—no bickering, no
second-guessing allowed! Go out into the world uncorrupted,
a breath of fresh air in this squalid and polluted society.
Provide people with a glimpse of good living and of the living
God. Carry the light-giving Message into the night.*

Philippians 2:14-15 MSG

God loves a cheerful giver.

2 Corinthians 9:7 NIV

more words of wisdom

Cheerfulness prepares a glorious mind for all the noblest acts of religion—love, adoration, praise, and every union with our God.

Elizabeth Ann Seton

Be assured, my dear friend, that it is no joy to God in seeing you with a dreary countenance.

C. H. Spurgeon

Sour godliness is the devil's religion.

John Wesley

**Hope is the power of being cheerful
in circumstances which we know to be desperate.**

G. K. Chesterton

-A Tip-

Cheer up somebody else. Do you need a little cheering up? If so, find somebody else who needs cheering up, too. Then, do your best to brighten that person's day. When you do, you'll discover that cheering up other people is a wonderful way to cheer yourself up, too!

God's Promises About...
CHOICES

But Daniel purposed in his heart that he would not defile himself . . . .

Daniel 1:8 KJV

I am offering you life or death, blessings or curses. Now, choose life! . . . To choose life is to love the Lord your God, obey him, and stay close to him.

Deuteronomy 30:19-20 NCV

So I strive always to keep my conscience clear before God and man.

Acts 24:16 NIV

**The thing you should want most is God's kingdom and doing what God wants.
Then all these other things you need will be given to you.**

Matthew 6:33 NCV

EXTREME

more words of wisdom

There may be no trumpet sound or loud applause when we make a right decision, just a calm sense of resolution and peace.

Gloria Gaither

We are either the masters or the victims of our attitudes. It is a matter of personal choice. Who we are today is the result of choices we made yesterday. Tomorrow, we will become what we choose today. To change means to choose to change.

John Maxwell

**The location of your affections
will drive the direction of your decisions.**

Lisa Bevere

I do not know how the Spirit of Christ performs it, but He brings us choices through which we constantly change, fresh and new, into His likeness.

Joni Eareckson Tada

-A Tip-

First you'll make choices . . . and before you know it, your choices will make you. So choose carefully.

God's Promises About...
CHRIST'S LOVE

I am the good shepherd. The good shepherd lays down his life for the sheep.

John 10:11 NIV

And remember, I am with you always, to the end of the age.

Matthew 28:20 HCSB

Who will separate us from the love of Christ? Will tribulation, or distress, or persecution, or famine, or nakedness, or peril, or sword? . . . But in all these things we overwhelmingly conquer through Him who loved us.

Romans 8:35, 37 NASB

But God demonstrates His own love toward us, in that while we were still sinners, Christ died for us.

Romans 5:8 NKJV

As the Father hath loved me, so have I loved you; continue ye in my love.

John 15:9 KJV

EXTREME

more words of wisdom

**Jesus is all compassion.
He never betrays us.**

Catherine Marshall

Live your lives in love, the same sort of love which Christ gives us, and which He perfectly expressed when He gave Himself as a sacrifice to God.

Corrie ten Boom

So Jesus came, stripping himself of everything as he came— omnipotence, omniscience, omnipresence—everything except love. "He emptied himself" (Philippians 2:7), emptied himself of everything except love. Love—his only protection, his only weapon, his only method.

E. Stanley Jones

-A Tip-

Jesus loves me, this I know . . . but how much? Here's how much: Jesus loves you so much that He gave His life so that you might live forever with Him in heaven. And how can you repay Christ's love? By accepting Him into your heart and by obeying His rules. When you do, He will love you and bless you today, tomorrow, and forever.

God's Promises About...
CHRIST'S SACRIFICE

Everyone has to die once, then face the consequences. Christ's death was also a one-time event, but it was a sacrifice that took care of sins forever. And so, when he next appears, the outcome for those eager to greet him is, precisely, salvation.

Hebrews 9:27-28 MSG

For Christ also died for sins once for all, the just for the unjust, so that He might bring us to God, having been put to death in the flesh, but made alive in the spirit.

1 Peter 3:18 NASB

For when we were still without strength, in due time Christ died for the ungodly.

Romans 5:6 NKJV

But now in Christ Jesus you who once were far off have been brought near by the blood of Christ. For He Himself is our peace.

Ephesians 2:13-14 NKJV

EXTREME

more words of wisdom

In his life, Christ is an example showing us how to live; in his death, he is a sacrifice satisfying for our sins.

Martin Luther

The cross means this: Jesus taking our place to satisfy the demands of God's justice and turning aside God's wrath.

James Montgomery Boice

The cross takes care of the past. The cross takes care of the flesh. The cross takes care of the world.

Kay Arthur

Jesus means Savior, revealing His God-ordained mission to present Himself as the Lamb, without spot or blemish, Who would make atonement for the sin of the world through the sacrifice of Himself on the altar of the cross.

Anne Graham Lotz

-A Tip-

When Jesus endured His sacrifice on the cross, He paid a terrible price for you. What price are you willing to pay for Him?

God's Promises About...
CHURCH

**Now you are the body of Christ,
and individual members of it.**

1 Corinthians 12:27 HCSB

And I also say to you that you are Peter, and on this rock I will build My church, and the forces of Hades will not overpower it. I will give you the keys of the kingdom of heaven, and whatever you bind on earth will have been bound in heaven, and whatever you loose on earth will have been loosed in heaven.

Matthew 16:18-19 HCSB

Don't you realize that all of you together are the temple of God and that the Spirit of God lives in you?

1 Corinthians 3:16 NLT

Be on guard for yourselves and for all the flock, among whom the Holy Spirit has appointed you as overseers, to shepherd the church of God, which He purchased with His own blood.

Acts 20:28 HCSB

Then He began to teach them: "Is it not written, My house will be called a house of prayer for all nations? But you have made it a den of thieves!"

Mark 11:17 HCSB

more words of wisdom

A living church gathers its members of all age groups and says, "Come! In this precious, unique, 'now' time, let's all go hard after God!"

Anne Ortlund

Our churches are meant to be havens where the caste rules of the world do not apply.

Beth Moore

To model the kingdom of God in the world, the church must not only be a repentant community, committed to truth, but also a holy community.

Chuck Colson

It has always been the work of the church to bring others to belief in Christ and to experience a personal relationship with Him.

Charles Stanley

-A Tip-

Make it a celebration, not an obligation: What you put into church determines what you get out of it. Your attitude towards worship is vitally important . . . so celebrate accordingly!

God's Promises About...
COMPASSION

**And let us be concerned about one another
in order to promote love and good works.**

Hebrews 10:24 HCSB

*Finally, all of you be of one mind, having compassion for one
another; love as brothers, be tenderhearted, be courteous.*

1 Peter 3:8 NKJV

*Therefore, God's chosen ones, holy and loved, put on heartfelt
compassion, kindness, humility, gentleness, and patience.*

Colossians 3:12 HCSB

*But he's already made it plain how to live, what to do, what
God is looking for in men and women. It's quite simple: Do
what is fair and just to your neighbor, be compassionate and
loyal in your love, and don't take yourself too seriously—take
God seriously.*

Micah 6:8 MSG

*I pray that your love for each other will overflow more and
more, and that you will keep on growing in your knowledge
and understanding.*

Philippians 1:9 NLT

EXTREME

more words of wisdom

Reach out and care for someone who needs the touch of hospitality. The time you spend caring today will be a love gift that will blossom into the fresh joy of God's Spirit in the future.

Emilie Barnes

**Let my heart be broken
by the things that break the heart of God.**

Bob Pierce

We must learn to regard people less in the light of what they do or do not do, and more in the light of what they suffer.

Dietrich Bonhoeffer

Compassion is sometimes the fatal capacity for feeling what it is like to live inside somebody else's skin. It is the knowledge that there can never really be any peace and joy for me until there is peace and joy finally for you too.

Frederick Buechner

-A Tip-

It's good to feel compassion for others . . . but it's better to do something for them! When in doubt, do the compassionate thing.

promises for life

God's Promises About...
COMPLAINING

Do everything without complaining or arguing. Then you will be innocent and without any wrong.

Philippians 2:14-15 NCV

Be hospitable to one another without complaining.

1 Peter 4:9 HCSB

Friends, don't complain about each other. A far greater complaint could be lodged against you, you know. The Judge is standing just around the corner.

James 5:9 MSG

May the words of my mouth and the thoughts of my heart be pleasing to you, O LORD, my rock and my redeemer.

Psalm 19:14 NLT

**Set a guard over my mouth, O LORD;
keep watch over the door of my lips.**

Psalm 141:3 NIV

EXTREME

more words of wisdom

Life is too short to nurse one's misery. Hurry across the lowlands so that you may spend more time on the mountaintops.

Phillips Brooks

Jesus wept, but he never complained.

C. H. Spurgeon

When you're on the verge of throwing a pity party thanks to your despairing thoughts, go back to the Word of God.

Charles Swindoll

It's your choice: you can either count your blessings or recount your disappointments.

Jim Gallery

He wants us to have a faith that does not complain while waiting, but rejoices because we know our times are in His hands—nail-scarred hands that labor for our highest good.

Kay Arthur

-A Tip-

Perpetual complaining is a bad habit, and it's contagious . . . make sure that your friends and family members don't catch it from you!

promises for life

God's Promises About...
CONFESSION

If you hide your sins, you will not succeed. If you confess and reject them, you will receive mercy.

Proverbs 28:13 NCV

If we confess our sins, He is faithful
and righteous to forgive us our sins
and to cleanse us from all unrighteousness.

1 John 1:9 HCSB

Make this your common practice: Confess your sins to each other and pray for each other so that you can live together whole and healed. The prayer of a person living right with God is something powerful to be reckoned with.

James 5:16 MSG

Pursue righteousness, godliness, faith, love, endurance, and gentleness. Fight the good fight for the faith; take hold of eternal life, to which you were called and have made a good confession before many witnesses.

1 Timothy 6:11-12 HCSB

Let us hold on to the confession of our hope without wavering, for He who promised is faithful.

Hebrews 10:23 HCSB

more words of wisdom

According to Psalm 66:18, you cannot even commune with God, let alone grow spiritually, if you are harboring sin. That's why confession is so vital.

John MacArthur

I can vividly remember times in my life when God seemed silent, and I realized He was waiting on me to confront and confess certain sins in my life.

Beth Moore

When we come to Jesus stripped of pretensions, with a needy spirit, ready to listen, He meets us at the point of need.

Catherine Marshall

There is nothing that God cannot forgive except for the rejection of Christ. No matter how black the sin, how hideous the sin, if we but confess it to Him in true repentance and faith, He will forgive. He will accept and forgive.

Ruth Bell Graham

-A Tip-

Confess your sin to God before you confess to anyone else.

promises for life

God's Promises About...
CONSCIENCE

I always do my best to have a clear conscience toward God and men.

Acts 24:16 HCSB

Now the goal of our instruction is love from a pure heart, a good conscience, and a sincere faith.

1 Timothy 1:5 HCSB

And do not be conformed to this world, but be transformed by the renewing of your mind, that you may prove what is that good and acceptable and perfect will of God.

Romans 12:2 NKJV

Let us draw near with a true heart in full assurance of faith, our hearts sprinkled clean from an evil conscience and our bodies washed in pure water.

Hebrews 10:22 HCSB

I will cling to my righteousness and never let it go. My conscience will not accuse [me] as long as I live!

Job 27:6 HCSB

EXTREME

more words of wisdom

God desires that we become spiritually healthy enough through faith to have a conscience that rightly interprets the work of the Holy Spirit.

Beth Moore

Your conscience is your alarm system. It's your protection.

Charles Stanley

If your conscience tells you to say no, then say it.

Criswell Freeman

Guilt is a gift that leads us to grace.

Franklin Graham

He that loses his conscience has nothing left that is worth keeping.

Izaak Walton

-A Tip-

Listening to that little voice . . . That quiet little voice inside your head will guide you down the right path if you listen carefully. Very often, your conscience will actually tell you what God wants you to do. So listen, learn, and behave accordingly.

48

God's Promises About...
CONTENTMENT

The LORD gives strength to his people; the LORD blesses his people with peace.

Psalm 29:11 NIV

**_I have learned to be content
in whatever circumstances I am._**

Philippians 4:11 HCSB

A tranquil heart is life to the body, but jealousy is rottenness to the bones.

Proverbs 14:30 HCSB

Serving God does make us very rich, if we are satisfied with what we have. We brought nothing into the world, so we can take nothing out. But, if we have food and clothes, we will be satisfied with that.

1 Timothy 6:6-8 NCV

Let your conduct be without covetousness; be content with such things as you have. For He Himself has said, "I will never leave you nor forsake you."

Hebrews 13:5 NKJV

more words of wisdom

The secret of contentment in the midst of change is found in having roots in the changeless Christ—the same yesterday, today and forever.

Ed Young

Nobody who gets enough food and clothing in a world where most are hungry and cold has any business to talk about "misery."

C. S. Lewis

Real contentment hinges on what's happening inside us, not around us.

Charles Stanley

Father and Mother lived on the edge of poverty, and yet their contentment was not dependent upon their surroundings. Their relationship to each other and to the Lord gave them strength and happiness.

Corrie ten Boom

-A Tip-

Contentment comes, not from your circumstances, but from your attitude.

God's Promises About...
CONVERSION

Jesus replied, "I assure you: Unless someone is born again, he cannot see the kingdom of God." "But how can anyone be born when he is old?" Nicodemus asked Him. "Can he enter his mother's womb a second time and be born?" Jesus answered, "I assure you: Unless someone is born of water and the Spirit, he cannot enter the kingdom of God."

John 3:3-5 HCSB

Whoever believes that Jesus is the Christ is born of God, and whoever loves the Father loves the child born of Him.

1 John 5:1 NASB

Your old life is dead. Your new life, which is your real life—even though invisible to spectators—is with Christ in God. He is your life.

Colossians 3:3 MSG

Then He called a child to Him and had him stand among them. "I assure you," He said, "unless you are converted and become like children, you will never enter the kingdom of heaven."

Matthew 18:2-3 HCSB

more words of wisdom

**Conversion is not a blind leap into the darkness.
It is a joyous leap into the light
that is the love of God.**

Corrie ten Boom

Being a Christian is more than just an instantaneous conversion; it is like a daily process whereby you grow to be more and more like Christ.

Billy Graham

If we accept His invitation to salvation, we live with Him forever. However, if we do not accept because we refuse His only Son as our Savior, then we exclude ourselves from My Father's House. It's our choice.

Anne Graham Lotz

Jesus divided people—everyone—into two classes—the once-born and the twice-born, the unconverted and the converted. No other distinction mattered.

E. Stanley Jones

-A Tip-

A true conversion results in a life transformed by Christ and a commitment to following in His footsteps.

promises for life

God's Promises About...
COURAGE

Be strong and courageous,
all you who put your hope in the LORD.

Psalm 31:24 HCSB

The LORD himself goes before you and will be with you; he will never leave you nor forsake you. Do not be afraid; do not be discouraged.

Deuteronomy 31:8 NIV

So do not fear, for I am with you; do not be dismayed, for I am your God. I will strengthen you and help you; I will uphold you with my righteous right hand.

Isaiah 41:10 NIV

But He said to them, "Why are you fearful, you of little faith?" Then He got up and rebuked the winds and the sea. And there was a great calm.

Matthew 8:26 HCSB

Wait for the LORD; be courageous and let your heart be strong. Wait for the LORD.

Psalm 27:14 HCSB

more words of wisdom

God did away with all my fear. It was time for someone to stand up—or in my case, sit down. So I refused to move.

Rosa Parks

Jesus Christ can make the weakest man into a divine dreadnought, fearing nothing.

Oswald Chambers

There comes a time when we simply have to face the challenges in our lives and stop backing down.

John Eldredge

Just as courage is faith in good, so discouragement is faith in evil, and, while courage opens the door to good, discouragement opens it to evil.

Hannah Whitall Smith

A man who is intimate with God will never be intimidated by men.

Leonard Ravenhill

-A Tip-

Courage is trusting God to handle the problems that are simply too big for you to solve.

promises for life

God's Promises About...
DEATH

And now, brothers and sisters, I want you to know what will happen to the Christians who have died so you will not be full of sorrow like people who have no hope.

1 Thessalonians 4:13 NLT

Death, where is your victory? Death, where is your pain? Death's power to hurt is sin, and the power of sin is the law. But we thank God! He gives us the victory through our Lord Jesus Christ.

1 Corinthians 15:55-57 NCV

The last enemy that will be destroyed is death.

1 Corinthians 15:26 NKJV

It has now been revealed through the appearing of our Savior, Christ Jesus, who has destroyed death and has brought life and immortality to light through the gospel.

2 Timothy 1:10 NIV

A good reputation is more valuable than the most expensive perfume. In the same way, the day you die is better than the day you are born.

Ecclesiastes 7:1 NLT

more words of wisdom

They that love beyond the world cannot be separated by it. Death cannot kill what never dies, nor can spirits ever be divided that love and live in the same divine principle.

William Penn

If we really think that home is elsewhere and that this life is a "wandering to find home," why should we not look forward to the arrival?

C. S. Lewis

Life is immortal, love eternal; death is nothing but a horizon, and a horizon is only the limit of our vision.

Corrie ten Boom

How we leave the world is more important than how we enter it.

Janette Oke

-A Tip-

Death is a fact of life, and nobody knows when or where it's going to happen. So when it comes to making plans for life here on earth and for life eternal, you'd better be ready to live—and to die—right now.

promises for life

God's Promises About...
DECISIONS

Now if any of you lacks wisdom, he should ask God, who gives to all generously and without criticizing, and it will be given to him. But let him ask in faith without doubting. For the doubter is like the surging sea, driven and tossed by the wind.

James 1:5-6 HCSB

But Daniel purposed in his heart that he would not defile himself . . . .

Daniel 1:8 KJV

I am offering you life or death, blessings or curses. Now, choose life! . . . To choose life is to love the Lord your God, obey him, and stay close to him.

Deuteronomy 30:19-20 NCV

Even zeal is not good without knowledge, and the one who acts hastily sins.

Proverbs 19:2 HCSB

But seek first the kingdom of God and His righteousness, and all these things will be provided for you.

Matthew 6:33 HCSB

more words of wisdom

No trumpets sound when the important decisions of our life are made. Destiny is made known silently.

Agnes DeMille

The Reference Point for the Christian is the Bible. All values, judgments, and attitudes must be gauged in relationship to this Reference Point.

Ruth Bell Graham

Successful people make right decisions early and manage those decisions daily.

John Maxwell

God always gives His best to those who leave the choice with Him.

Jim Elliot

-A Tip-

Think first! Think before you say things . . . and think before you do things. Otherwise, you can get yourself in trouble. So here's a good rule to follow: Slow down long enough to think about the things you're about to do or say. That way, you'll make better choices.

promises for life

God's Promises About...
DIFFICULT DAYS

We also have joy with our troubles, because we know that these troubles produce patience. And patience produces character, and character produces hope.

Romans 5:3-4 NCV

We take the good days from God—why not also the bad days?

Job 2:10 MSG

**We are hard pressed on every side,
yet not crushed; we are perplexed,
but not in despair.**

2 Corinthians 4:8 NKJV

A time to weep, and a time to laugh; a time to mourn, and a time to dance . . . .

Ecclesiastes 3:4 KJV

They do not fear bad news; they confidently trust the LORD to care for them. They are confident and fearless and can face their foes triumphantly.

Psalm 112:7-8 NLT

more words of wisdom

The strengthening of faith comes from staying with it in the hour of trial. We should not shrink from tests of faith.

Catherine Marshall

Our heavenly Father never takes anything from his children unless he means to give them something better.

George Mueller

Even in the winter, even in the midst of the storm, the sun is still there. Somewhere, up above the clouds, it still shines and warms and pulls at the life buried deep inside the brown branches and frozen earth. The sun is there! Spring will come.

Gloria Gaither

When life is difficult, God wants us to have a faith that trusts and waits.

Kay Arthur

-A Tip-

Difficult days come and go. Stay the course. The sun is shining somewhere and will soon shine on you.

promises for life

God's Promises About...
DISCIPLESHIP

You did not choose Me, but I chose you. I appointed you that you should go out and produce fruit, and that your fruit should remain, so that whatever you ask the Father in My name, He will give you.

John 15:16 HCSB

**Be imitators of God, therefore,
as dearly loved children.**

Ephesians 5:1 NIV

Work hard, but not just to please your masters when they are watching. As slaves of Christ, do the will of God with all your heart. Work with enthusiasm, as though you were working for the Lord rather than for people.

Ephesians 6:6-7 NLT

But whoever keeps His word, truly in him the love of God is perfected. This is how we know we are in Him: the one who says he remains in Him should walk just as He walked.

1 John 2:5-6 HCSB

We encouraged, comforted, and implored each one of you to walk worthy of God, who calls you into His own kingdom and glory.

1 Thessalonians 2:12 HCSB

more words of wisdom

It is the secret of true discipleship to bear the cross, to acknowledge the death sentence that has been passed on self, and to deny any right that self has to rule over us.

Andrew Murray

When Jesus put the little child in the midst of His disciples, He did not tell the little child to become like His disciples; He told the disciples to become like the little child.

Ruth Bell Graham

**A believer comes to Christ;
a disciple follows after Him.**

Vance Havner

The great stumbling block in the way of some people being disciples is that they are gifted, so gifted that they won't trust God.

Oswald Chambers

-A Tip-

Talk is cheap. Real ministry has legs. When it comes to being a disciple, make sure that you back up your words with deeds.

God's Promises About...
DISCIPLINE

No discipline seems enjoyable at the time, but painful. Later on, however, it yields the fruit of peace and righteousness to those who have been trained by it.

Hebrews 12:11 HCSB

For this very reason, make every effort to supplement your faith with goodness, goodness with knowledge, knowledge with self-control, self-control with endurance, endurance with godliness.

2 Peter 1:5-6 HCSB

Whoever gives heed to instruction prospers, and blessed is he that trusts in the LORD.

Proverbs 16:20 NIV

**The one who follows instruction
is on the path to life,
but the one who rejects correction goes astray.**

Proverbs 10:17 HCSB

I discipline my body and bring it under strict control, so that after preaching to others, I myself will not be disqualified.

1 Corinthians 9:27 HCSB

more words of wisdom

Real freedom means to welcome the responsibility it brings, to welcome the God-control it requires, to welcome the discipline that results, to welcome the maturity it creates.

Eugenia Price

Discipline is training that develops and corrects.

Charles Stanley

True willpower and courage are not on the battlefield, but in everyday conquests over our inertia, laziness, and boredom.

D. L. Moody

Work is doing it. Discipline is doing it every day. Diligence is doing it well every day.

Dave Ramsey

Man's great danger is the combination of his increased control over the elements and his lack of control over himself.

Albert Schweitzer

-A Tip-

A disciplined lifestyle gives you more control: The more disciplined you become, the more you can take control over your life (which, by the way, is far better than letting your life take control over you).

God's Promises About...
DOUBTS

Purify your hearts, ye double-minded.

James 4:8 KJV

**When doubts filled my mind,
your comfort gave me renewed hope and cheer.**

Psalm 94:19 NLT

Then He said to Thomas, "Put your finger here and observe My hands. Reach out your hand and put it into My side. Don't be an unbeliever, but a believer."

John 20:27 HCSB

Immediately the father of the child cried out and said with tears, "Lord, I believe; help my unbelief!"

Mark 9:24 NKJV

So He said, "Come." And when Peter had come down out of the boat, he walked on the water to go to Jesus. But when he saw that the wind was boisterous, he was afraid; and beginning to sink he cried out, saying, "Lord, save me!" And immediately Jesus stretched out His hand and caught him, and said to him, "O you of little faith, why did you doubt?" And when they got into the boat, the wind ceased.

Matthew 14:29-32 NKJV

EXTREME

more words of wisdom

Struggling with God over the issues of life doesn't show a lack of faith—that is faith.

Lee Strobel

Unconfessed sin in your life will cause you to doubt.

Anne Graham Lotz

**Doubting may temporarily disturb,
but will not permanently destroy,
your faith in Christ.**

Charles Swindoll

The Holy Spirit is no skeptic, and the things he has written in our hearts are not doubts or opinions, but assertions—surer and more certain than sense or life itself.

Martin Luther

To wrestle with God does not mean that we have lost faith, but that we are fighting for it.

Sheila Walsh

-A Tip-

When you have doubts, it is important to take those doubts to the Lord.

promises for life

GOd's Promises About...
ENCOURAGEMENT

**Therefore encourage one another
and build each other up
as you are already doing.**

1 Thessalonians 5:11 HCSB

But encourage each other daily, while it is still called today, so that none of you is hardened by sin's deception.

Hebrews 3:13 HCSB

And let us be concerned about one another in order to promote love and good works.

Hebrews 10:24 HCSB

I want their hearts to be encouraged and joined together in love, so that they may have all the riches of assured understanding, and have the knowledge of God's mystery—Christ.

Colossians 2:2 HCSB

Carry one another's burdens; in this way you will fulfill the law of Christ.

Galatians 6:2 HCSB

more words of wisdom

Giving encouragement to others is a most welcome gift, for the results of it are lifted spirits, increased self-worth, and a hopeful future.

Florence Littauer

I can usually sense that a leading is from the Holy Spirit when it calls me to humble myself, to serve somebody, to encourage somebody, or to give something away. Very rarely will the evil one lead us to do those kind of things.

Bill Hybels

The secret of success is to find a need and fill it, to find a hurt and heal it, to find somebody with a problem and offer to help solve it.

Robert Schuller

-A Tip-

Do you want to be successful and go far in life? Encourage others to do the same. You can't lift other people up without lifting yourself up, too. And remember the words of Oswald Chambers: "God grant that we may not hinder those who are battling their way slowly into the light."

God's Promises About...
ENTHUSIASM

Whatever work you do, do your best, because you are going to the grave, where there is no working . . . .

Ecclesiastes 9:10 NCV

Whatever you do, do it enthusiastically, as something done for the Lord and not for men.

Colossians 3:23 HCSB

**Never be lazy in your work,
but serve the Lord enthusiastically.**

Romans 12:11 NLT

I have seen that there is nothing better than for a person to enjoy his activities, because that is his reward. For who can enable him to see what will happen after he dies?

Ecclesiastes 3:22 HCSB

Do your work with enthusiasm. Work as if you were serving the Lord, not as if you were serving only men and women.

Ephesians 6:7 NCV

EXTREME

more words of wisdom

We act as though comfort and luxury were the chief requirements of life, when all we need to make us really happy is something to be enthusiastic about.

Charles Kingsley

Get absolutely enthralled with something. Throw yourself into it with abandon. Get out of yourself. Be somebody. Do something.

Norman Vincent Peale

Wherever you are, be all there.
Live to the hilt every situation
you believe to be the will of God.

Jim Elliot

-A Tip-

Be enthusiastic about your faith: John Wesley wrote, "You don't have to advertise a fire. Get on fire for God and the world will come to watch you burn." When you allow yourself to become extremely enthusiastic about your faith, other people will notice—and so will God.

God's Promises About...
ETERNAL LIFE

And this is the testimony: God has given us eternal life, and this life is in His Son. The one who has the Son has life. The one who doesn't have the Son of God does not have life.

1 John 5:11-12 HCSB

Jesus said to her, "I am the resurrection and the life. The one who believes in Me, even if he dies, will live. Everyone who lives and believes in Me will never die—ever. Do you believe this?"

John 11:25-26 HCSB

I have written these things to you who believe in the name of the Son of God, so that you may know that you have eternal life.

1 John 5:13 HCSB

Pursue righteousness, godliness, faith, love, endurance, and gentleness. Fight the good fight for the faith; take hold of eternal life, to which you were called and have made a good confession before many witnesses.

1 Timothy 6:11-12 HCSB

EXTREME

more words of wisdom

Those of us who know the wonderful grace of redemption look forward to an eternity with God, when all things will be made new, when all our longings will at last find ultimate and final satisfaction.

Joseph Stowell

**And because we know Christ is alive,
we have hope for the present
and hope for life beyond the grave.**

Billy Graham

Once a man is united to God, how could he not live forever? Once a man is separated from God, what can he do but wither and die?

C. S. Lewis

Christ is the only liberator whose liberation lasts forever.

Malcolm Muggeridge

-A Tip-

You have a responsibility to tell as many people as you can about the eternal life that Jesus offers.

promises for life

God's Promises About...
EVIL

You were taught to leave your old self—to stop living the evil way you lived before. That old self becomes worse, because people are fooled by the evil things they want to do. But you were taught to be made new in your hearts, to become a new person. That new person is made to be like God—made to be truly good and holy.

Ephesians 4:22-24 NCV

Be sober! Be on the alert! Your adversary the Devil is prowling around like a roaring lion, looking for anyone he can devour.

1 Peter 5:8 HCSB

This High Priest of ours understands our weaknesses, for he faced all of the same temptations we do, yet he did not sin.

Hebrews 4:15 NLT

Submit yourselves therefore to God. Resist the devil, and he will flee from you. Draw nigh to God, and he will draw nigh to you.

James 4:7-8 KJV

Be not wise in thine own eyes:
fear the Lord, and depart from evil.

Proverbs 3:7 KJV

more words of wisdom

The only thing necessary for the triumph of evil is for good men to do nothing.

Edmund Burke

Of two evils, choose neither.

C. H. Spurgeon

Evil is that which God does not will.

Emil Brunner

There is but one good; that is God. Everything else is good when it looks to Him and bad when it turns from Him.

C. S. Lewis

We are in a continual battle with the spiritual forces of evil, but we will triumph when we yield to God's leading and call on His powerful presence in prayer.

Shirley Dobson

-A Tip-

There is darkness in this world, but God's light can overpower any darkness.

promises for life

God's Promises About...
EXAMPLE

Do everything without grumbling and arguing, so that you may be blameless and pure.

Philippians 2:14-15 HCSB

We have around us many people whose lives tell us what faith means. So let us run the race that is before us and never give up. We should remove from our lives anything that would get in the way and the sin that so easily holds us back.

Hebrews 12:1 NCV

You are the light that gives light to the world . . . . In the same way, you should be a light for other people. Live so that they will see the good things you do and will praise your Father in heaven.

Matthew 5:14, 16 NCV

**Set an example of good works yourself,
with integrity and dignity in your teaching.**

Titus 2:7 HCSB

For the kingdom of God is not in talk but in power.

1 Corinthians 4:20 HCSB

EXTREME

more words of wisdom

There is a transcendent power in example. We reform others unconsciously when we walk uprightly.

Anne Sophie Swetchine

We urgently need people who encourage and inspire us to move toward God and away from the world's enticing pleasures.

Jim Cymbala

In our faith we follow in someone's steps. In our faith we leave footprints to guide others. It's the principle of discipleship.

Max Lucado

Living life with a consistent spiritual walk deeply influences those we love most.

Vonette Bright

A man ought to live so that everybody knows he is a Christian, and most of all, his family ought to know.

D. L. Moody

-A Tip-

Your life is a sermon . . . What kind of sermon will you preach? The words you choose to speak may have some impact on others, but not nearly as much impact as the life you choose to live.

promises for life

God's Promises About...
EXPERIENCE

When a wise man is instructed, he gains knowledge.

Proverbs 21:11 NIV

Happy is the man who finds wisdom, and the man who gains understanding.

Proverbs 3:13 NKJV

No wisdom, no understanding, and no counsel [will prevail] against the LORD.

Proverbs 21:30 HCSB

A mocker seeks wisdom and doesn't find it, but knowledge [comes] easily to the perceptive.

Proverbs 14:6 HCSB

**Take good counsel and accept correction—
that's the way to live wisely and well.**

Proverbs 19:20 MSG

EXTREME

more words of wisdom

The Gospel has to be experienced, not argued!

Grady Nutt

**While it is wise to learn from experience,
it is wiser to learn from the experience of others.**

Rick Warren

Any patch of sunlight in a wood will show you something about the sun which you could never get from reading books on astronomy. These pure and spontaneous pleasures are "patches of Godlight" in the woods of our experience.

C. S. Lewis

It is never enough to know about spiritual things with your mind. Mental knowledge is not the same thing as truly understanding from the center of your being, which results from experiencing and doing.

St. Teresa of Avila

-A Tip-

Use your experiences—both good and bad—to learn, to grow, to share, and to teach.

GOd's Promises About...
FAILURE

**If you listen to constructive criticism,
you will be at home among the wise.**

Proverbs 15:31 NLT

If we confess our sins to him, he is faithful and just to forgive us and to cleanse us from every wrong.

1 John 1:9 NLT

If you hide your sins, you will not succeed. If you confess and reject them, you will receive mercy.

Proverbs 28:13 NCV

So we're not giving up. How could we! Even though on the outside it often looks like things are falling apart on us, on the inside, where God is making new life, not a day goes by without his unfolding grace.

2 Corinthians 4:16 MSG

I waited patiently for the LORD; he turned to me and heard my cry. He lifted me out of the slimy pit, out of the mud and mire; he set my feet on a rock and gave me a firm place to stand. He put a new song in my mouth, a hymn of praise to our God . . . .

Psalm 40:1-3 NIV

EXTREME

more words of wisdom

If I'm not free to fail, I'm not free to take risks. And everything in life that's worth doing involves a willingness to take a risk and involves the risk of failure. I have to try, but I do not have to succeed.

Madeleine L'Engle

So you have failed? You have not failed; you have gained experience. Go forward!

Josemaria Escriva

The enemy of our souls loves to taunt us with past failures, wrongs, disappointments, disasters, and calamities. And if we let him continue doing this, our life becomes a long and dark tunnel, with very little light at the end.

Charles Swindoll

God is a specialist; He is well able to work our failures into His plans. Often the doorway to success is entered through the hallway of failure.

Erwin Lutzer

-A Tip-

Failure is never permanent . . . unless you give up and quit trying.

God's Promises About...
FAITH

Be alert, stand firm in the faith, be brave and strong.

1 Corinthians 16:13 HCSB

For whatever is born of God overcomes the world. And this is the victory that has overcome the world—our faith.

1 John 5:4 NKJV

It is impossible to please God apart from faith. And why? Because anyone who wants to approach God must believe both that he exists and that he cares enough to respond to those who seek him.

Hebrews 11:6 MSG

For we walk by faith, not by sight.

2 Corinthians 5:7 HCSB

Now faith is the reality of what is hoped for, the proof of what is not seen.

Hebrews 11:1 HCSB

EXTREME

more words of wisdom

A faith that hasn't been tested can't be trusted.

Adrian Rogers

There are a lot of things in life that are difficult to understand. Faith allows the soul to go beyond what the eyes can see.

John Maxwell

The popular idea of faith is of a certain obstinate optimism: the hope, tenaciously held in the face of trouble, that the universe is fundamentally friendly and things may get better.

J. I. Packer

**Faith is our spiritual oxygen.
It not only keeps us alive in God,
but enables us to grow stronger . . . .**

Joyce Landorf Heatherly

-A Tip-

Faith in God is contagious . . . and when it comes to your family's spiritual journey, no one's faith is more contagious than yours! Act, pray, praise, and trust God with the certain knowledge that your friends and family are watching . . . carefully!

promises for life

God's Promises About...
FEAR

Indeed, God is my salvation. I will trust [Him] and not be afraid.

Isaiah 12:2 HCSB

Don't be afraid, because the Lord your God will be with you everywhere you go.

Joshua 1:9 NCV

Be strong and courageous, and do the work. Do not be afraid or discouraged, for the LORD God, my God, is with you.

1 Chronicles 28:20 NIV

I leave you peace; my peace I give you. I do not give it to you as the world does. So don't let your hearts be troubled or afraid.

John 14:27 NCV

In my anguish I cried to the LORD, and he answered by setting me free. The LORD is with me; I will not be afraid. What can man do to me?

Psalm 118:5-6 NIV

more words of wisdom

Are you fearful? First, bow your head and pray for God's strength. Then, raise your head and look Old Man Trouble squarely in the eye. Chances are, Old Man Trouble will blink.

Jim Gallery

Whether our fear is absolutely realistic or out of proportion in our minds, our greatest refuge is Jesus Christ.

Luci Swindoll

Courage faces fear and thereby masters it. Cowardice represses fear and is thereby mastered by it.

Martin Luther King, Jr.

I have found the perfect antidote for fear.
Whenever it sticks up its ugly face,
I clobber it with prayer.

Dale Evans Rogers

-A Tip-

Are you feeling anxious or fearful? If so, trust God to handle those problems that are simply too big for you to solve. Entrust the future—your future—to God.

promises for life

GOd's Promises About...
FELLOWSHIP

The one who loves his brother remains in the light, and there is no cause for stumbling in him.

1 John 2:10 HCSB

**You must get along with each other.
You must learn to be considerate of one another,
cultivating a life in common.**

1 Corinthians 1:10 MSG

Don't become partners with those who reject God. How can you make a partnership out of right and wrong? That's not partnership; that's war. Is light best friends with dark?

2 Corinthians 6:14 MSG

Now finally, all of you should be like-minded and sympathetic, should love believers, and be compassionate and humble.

1 Peter 3:8 HCSB

Therefore, as we have opportunity, we must work for the good of all, especially for those who belong to the household of faith.

Galatians 6:10 HCSB

more words of wisdom

Christians are like the flowers in a garden: they have upon them the dew of heaven, which, being shaken by the wind, they let fall at each other's roots, whereby they are jointly nourished.

John Bunyan

Be united with other Christians. A wall with loose bricks is not good. The bricks must be cemented together.

Corrie ten Boom

The Lord Jesus Christ enables us all to be family.

Dennis Swanberg

Your life together with other believers stands as the best confirmation that you know God.

Stanley Grenz

-A Tip-

Christians are not Lone Rangers. They are members of a spiritual family, and they need one another.

God's Promises About...
FINANCES

Honor the Lord with your wealth and the firstfruits from all your crops. Then your barns will be full, and your wine barrels will overflow with new wine.

Proverbs 3:9-10 NCV

And my God shall supply all your need according to His riches in glory by Christ Jesus.

Philippians 4:19 NKJV

Then she came and told the man of God. And he said, "Go, sell the oil and pay your debt; and you and your sons live on the rest."

2 Kings 4:7 NKJV

Do not co-sign another person's note or put up a guarantee for someone else's loan. If you can't pay it, even your bed will be snatched from under you.

Proverbs 22:26 NLT

EXTREME

more words of wisdom

Here's a recipe for handling money wisely: Take a heaping helping of common sense, add a sizeable portion of self-discipline, and mix with prayer.

Marie T. Freeman

A Christian who is not experiencing the peace and fulfillment in financial matters that the Bible promises is in bondage.

Larry Burkett

**If you work hard and maintain
an attitude of gratitude, you'll find it easier
to manage your finances every day.**

John Maxwell

I sincerely believe that once Christians have been educated in God's plan for their finances, they will find a freedom they had never known before.

Larry Burkett

-A Tip-

Don't fall in love with "stuff." We live in a society that worships "stuff"—don't fall into that trap. Remember this: "stuff" is highly overrated. Worship God almighty, not the almighty dollar. (Proverbs 11:28)

God's Promises About...
FOLLOWING CHRIST

We encouraged, comforted, and implored each one of you to walk worthy of God, who calls you into His own kingdom and glory.

1 Thessalonians 2:12 HCSB

Then he told them what they could expect for themselves: "Anyone who intends to come with me has to let me lead."

Luke 9:23 MSG

I've laid down a pattern for you.
What I've done, you do.

John 13:15 MSG

The one who loves his life will lose it, and the one who hates his life in this world will keep it for eternal life. If anyone serves Me, he must follow Me. Where I am, there My servant also will be. If anyone serves Me, the Father will honor him.

John 12:25-26 HCSB

Follow Me, Jesus told them, "and I will make you into fishers of men!" Immediately they left their nets and followed Him.

Mark 1:17-18 HCSB

more words of wisdom

Living life with a consistent spiritual walk deeply influences those we love most.

Vonette Bright

The cross that Jesus commands you and me to carry is the cross of submissive obedience to the will of God, even when His will includes suffering and hardship and things we don't want to do.

Anne Graham Lotz

**We have in Jesus Christ a perfect example
of how to put God's truth into practice.**

Bill Bright

A disciple is a follower of Christ. That means you take on His priorities as your own. His agenda becomes your agenda. His mission becomes your mission.

Charles Stanley

-A Tip-

If you want to follow in Christ's footsteps . . . welcome Him into your heart, obey His commandments, and share His never-ending love.

promises for life

God's Promises About...
FORGIVENESS

If you forgive those who sin against you, your heavenly Father will forgive you. But if you refuse to forgive others, your Father will not forgive your sins.

Matthew 6:14-15 NLT

Be even-tempered, content with second place, quick to forgive an offense. Forgive as quickly and completely as the Master forgave you. And regardless of what else you put on, wear love. It's your basic, all-purpose garment. Never be without it.

Colossians 3:13-14 MSG

And forgive us our sins, for we ourselves also forgive everyone in debt to us. And do not bring us into temptation.

Luke 11:4 NKJV

And be ye kind one to another, tenderhearted, forgiving one another, even as God for Christ's sake hath forgiven you.

Ephesians 4:32 KJV

Whenever you stand praying, forgive, if you have anything against anyone, so that your Father in heaven will also forgive you your transgressions.

Mark 11:25 NASB

EXTREME

more words of wisdom

As you have received the mercy of God by the forgiveness of sin and the promise of eternal life, thus you must show mercy.

Billy Graham

Only the truly forgiven are truly forgiving.

C. S. Lewis

Our relationships with other people are of primary importance to God. Because God is love, He cannot tolerate any unforgiveness or hardness in us toward any individual.

Catherine Marshall

But perhaps all peacemaking must begin in a similar spot—in prayer to God, interceding for another, asking blessing for the one who has cursed us, and opening our own hearts for godly examination.

Debra Evans

-A Tip-

Forgive . . . and keep forgiving! Sometimes, you may forgive someone once and then, at a later time, become angry at the very same person again. If so, you must forgive that person again and again . . . until it sticks!

promises for life

GOd's Promises About...
FRIENDS

Greater love has no one than this, that he lay down his life for his friends.

John 15:13 NIV

**If a fellow believer hurts you, go and tell him—
work it out between the two of you.
If he listens, you've made a friend.**

Matthew 18:15 MSG

Beloved, if God so loved us, we also ought to love one another.

1 John 4:11 NKJV

I thank my God upon every remembrance of you.

Philippians 1:3 NKJV

A friend loves at all times, and a brother is born for adversity.

Proverbs 17:17 NIV

EXTREME

more words of wisdom

**Friendships are living organisms at work.
They continue to unfold, change, and emerge.**

Barbara Johnson

The glory of friendship is not the outstretched hand, or the kindly smile, or the joy of companionship. It is the spiritual inspiration that comes to one when he discovers that someone else believes in him and is willing to trust him with his friendship.

Corrie ten Boom

In friendship, God opens your eyes to the glories of Himself.

Joni Eareckson Tada

Don't bypass the potential for meaningful friendships just because of differences. Explore them. Embrace them. Love them.

Luci Swindoll

-A Tip-

Remember the first rule of friendship: it's the Golden one, and it starts like this: "Do unto others . . ." (Matthew 7:12).

God's Promises About...
FUTURE

"I say this because I know what I am planning for you," says the Lord. "I have good plans for you, not plans to hurt you. I will give you hope and a good future."

Jeremiah 29:11 NCV

What a God we have! And how fortunate we are to have him, this Father of our Master Jesus! Because Jesus was raised from the dead, we've been given a brand-new life and have everything to live for, including a future in heaven—and the future starts now!

1 Peter 1:3-4 MSG

But if we hope for what we do not see, we eagerly wait for it with patience.

Romans 8:25 HCSB

Wisdom is pleasing to you. If you find it, you have hope for the future.

Proverbs 24:14 NCV

EXTREME

more words of wisdom

Do not limit the limitless God! With Him, face the future unafraid because you are never alone.

Mrs. Charles E. Cowman

No matter how heavy the burden, daily strength is given, so I expect we need not give ourselves any concern as to what the outcome will be. We must simply go forward.

Annie Armstrong

We spend our lives dreaming of the future, not realizing that a little of it slips away every day.

Barbara Johnson

The Christian believes in a fabulous future.

Billy Graham

Joy comes from knowing God loves me and knows who I am and where I'm going . . . that my future is secure as I rest in Him.

James Dobson

-A Tip-

Focus more on your future opportunities than on your past disappointments.

GOd's Promises About...
GENEROSITY

Above all, love each other deeply, because love covers a multitude of sins.

1 Peter 4:8 NIV

Now this I say, he who sows sparingly will also reap sparingly, and he who sows bountifully will also reap bountifully. Each one must do just as he has purposed in his heart, not grudgingly or under compulsion, for God loves a cheerful giver.

2 Corinthians 9:6-7 NASB

In every way I've shown you that by laboring like this, it is necessary to help the weak and to keep in mind the words of the Lord Jesus, for He said, "It is more blessed to give than to receive."

Acts 20:35 HCSB

The man with two tunics should share with him who has none, and the one who has food should do the same.

Luke 3:11 NIV

I tell you the truth, whatever you did for one of the least of these brothers of mine, you did for me.

Matthew 25:40 NIV

more words of wisdom

God does not supply money to satisfy our every whim and desire. His promise is to meet our needs and provide an abundance so that we can help other people.

Larry Burkett

The limit of giving is to be the limit of our ability to give.

C. S. Lewis

We are never more like God than when we give.

Charles Swindoll

The happiest and most joyful people are those who give money and serve.

Dave Ramsey

A cup that is already full cannot have more added to it. In order to receive the further good to which we are entitled, we must give of that which we have.

Margaret Becker

-A Tip-

Would you like to be a little happier? Try sharing a few more of the blessings that God has bestowed upon you. In other words, if you want to be happy, be generous. And if you want to be unhappy, be greedy.

promises for life

God's Promises About...
GRATITUDE

As you therefore have received Christ Jesus the Lord, so walk in Him, having been firmly rooted and now being built up in Him and established in your faith, just as you were instructed, and overflowing with gratitude.

Colossians 2:6-7 NASB

Everything created by God is good, and nothing is to be rejected, if it is received with gratitude; for it is sanctified by means of the word of God and prayer.

1 Timothy 4:4-5 NASB

Be cheerful no matter what; pray all the time; thank God no matter what happens. This is the way God wants you who belong to Christ Jesus to live.

1 Thessalonians 5:16-18 MSG

Therefore, since we receive a kingdom which cannot be shaken, let us show gratitude, by which we may offer to God an acceptable service with reverence and awe . . . .

Hebrews 12:28 NASB

I will praise the name of God with a song, and will magnify him with thanksgiving.

Psalm 69:30 KJV

EXTREME

more words of wisdom

We become happy, spiritually prosperous people not because we receive what we want, but because we appreciate what we have.

Penelope Stokes

Contentment comes when we develop an attitude of gratitude for the important things we do have in our lives that we tend to take for granted if we have our eyes staring longingly at our neighbor's stuff.

Dave Ramsey

If you won't fill your heart with gratitude, the devil will fill it with something else.

Marie T. Freeman

It is only with gratitude that life becomes rich.

Dietrich Bonhoeffer

-A Tip-

Developing an attitude of gratitude is key to a joyful and satisfying life.

God's Promises About...
GREED

For the love of money is a root of all sorts of evil, and some by longing for it have wandered away from the faith and pierced themselves with many griefs. But flee from these things, you man of God, and pursue righteousness, godliness, faith, love, perseverance and gentleness.

1 Timothy 6:11 NASB

Do not love the world or the things in the world. If anyone loves the world, the love of the Father is not in him.

1 John 2:15 NKJV

Such are the paths of all who pursue gain dishonestly; it takes the lives of those who profit from it.

Proverbs 1:19 HCSB

Your life should be free from the love of money. Be satisfied with what you have, for He Himself has said, I will never leave you or forsake you.

Hebrews 13:5 HCSB

EXTREME

more words of wisdom

Greed is enslaving. The more you have, the more you want— until eventually avarice consumes you.

Kay Arthur

The Scriptures also reveal warning that if we are consumed with greed, not only do we disobey God, but we will miss the opportunity to allow Him to use us as instruments for others.

Charles Stanley

The gaining of wealth as an end in itself is a very poor investment of a life. It requires a great deal of time—to the virtual exclusion of everything else including family, friends, hobbies, and relaxation.

Larry Burkett

**A person who hungers for money
will starve to death spiritually!**

Anonymous

-A Tip-

A greedy lifestyle is never fulfilling because greed leads to a constant (and unsuccessful) attempt to find happiness and abundance apart from God.

God's Promises About...
HAPPINESS

But the truly happy person is the one who carefully studies God's perfect law that makes people free. He continues to study it. He listens to God's teaching and does not forget what he heard. Then he obeys what God's teaching says. When he does this, it makes him happy.

James 1:25 ICB

I've learned by now to be quite content whatever my circumstances. I'm just as happy with little as with much, with much as with little. I've found the recipe for being happy whether full or hungry, hands full or hands empty.

Philippians 4:11-12 MSG

Always be happy. Never stop praying. Give thanks whatever happens. That is what God wants for you in Christ Jesus.

1 Thessalonians 5:16-18 ICB

Happy are those who fear the LORD. Yes, happy are those who delight in doing what he commands.

Psalm 112:1 NLT

**Delight thyself also in the LORD;
and he shall give thee the desires of thine heart.**

Psalm 37:4 KJV

more words of wisdom

**When we bring sunshine into the lives of others,
we're warmed by it ourselves.
When we spill a little happiness,
it splashes on us.**

Barbara Johnson

God has charged Himself with full responsibility for our eternal happiness and stands ready to take over the management of our lives the moment we turn in faith to Him.

A. W. Tozer

If you want to be truly happy, you won't find it on an endless quest for more stuff. You'll find it in receiving God's generosity and in passing that generosity along.

Bill Hybels

-A Tip-

Sometimes happy, sometimes not: Even if you're a very good person, you shouldn't expect to be happy all the time. Sometimes, things will happen to make you sad, and it's okay to be sad when bad things happen to you or to your friends and family. But remember: through good times and bad, you'll always be happier if you obey the rules of your Father in heaven. So obey them!

God's Promises About...
HEAVEN

Be glad and rejoice,
because your reward is great in heaven.

Matthew 5:12 HCSB

Let not your heart be troubled: ye believe in God, believe also in me. In my Father's house are many mansions: if it were not so, I would have told you. I go to prepare a place for you. And if I go and prepare a place for you, I will come again, and receive you unto myself; that where I am, there ye may be also.

John 14:1-3 KJV

He also raised us up with Him and seated us with Him in the heavens, in Christ Jesus, so that in the coming ages He might display the immeasurable riches of His grace in His kindness to us in Christ Jesus.

Ephesians 2:6-7 HCSB

Our citizenship is in heaven, from which we also eagerly wait for a Savior, the Lord Jesus Christ.

Philippians 3:20 HCSB

more words of wisdom

One of these days, our Father will scoop us up in His strong arms and we will hear Him say those sweet and comforting words, "Come on, child. We're going home."

Gloria Gaither

**Wrapped in His loving embrace,
we will sense peace, delight, assurance,
abundant love, warm fellowship,
total security, and absolute calm.**

Bill Bright

The believing Christian has hope as he stands at the grave of a loved one who is with the Lord, for he knows that the separation is not forever. It is a glorious truth that those who are in Christ never see each other for the last time.

Billy Graham

-A Tip-

Heaven is all those wonderful things you wish you had on earth . . . and infinitely more.

God's Promises About...
HIS FAITHFULNESS

Because of the LORD's great love we are not consumed, for his compassions never fail. They are new every morning; great is your faithfulness.

Lamentations 3:22-23 NIV

God is faithful, by whom you were called into the fellowship of His Son, Jesus Christ our Lord.

1 Corinthians 1:9 NKJV

I will sing of the tender mercies of the LORD forever! Young and old will hear of your faithfulness. Your unfailing love will last forever. Your faithfulness is as enduring as the heavens.

Psalm 89:1-2 NLT

For the LORD is good. His unfailing love continues forever, and his faithfulness continues to each generation.

Psalm 100:5 NLT

Blessed is he whose help is the God of Jacob, whose hope is in the LORD his God, the Maker of heaven and earth, the sea, and everything in them—the LORD, who remains faithful forever.

Psalm 146:5-6 NIV

more words of wisdom

God does not want to be a divine lifeguard who is summoned only in emergencies. He wants to be involved in every aspect of our lives.

Warren Wiersbe

With each new experience of letting God be in control, we gain courage and reinforcement for daring to do it again and again.

Gloria Gaither

And in truth, if we only knew it, our chief fitness is our utter helplessness. His strength is made perfect, not in our strength, but in our weakness. Our strength is only a hindrance.

Hannah Whitall Smith

**God's faithfulness and grace
makes the impossible possible.**

Sheila Walsh

-A Tip-

You can count on God to fulfill His every promise to you.

promises for life

God's Promises About...
HIS FORGIVENESS

It will be hard when all these things happen to you. But after that you will come back to the Lord your God and obey him, because the Lord your God is a merciful God. He will not leave you or destroy you. He will not forget the Agreement with your ancestors, which he swore to them.

Deuteronomy 4:30-31 NCV

Praise be to the God and Father of our Lord Jesus Christ! In his great mercy he has given us new birth into a living hope through the resurrection of Jesus Christ from the dead.

1 Peter 1:3 NIV

So let us come boldly to the throne of our gracious God. There we will receive his mercy, and we will find grace to help us when we need it.

Hebrews 4:16 NLT

But God's mercy is great, and he loved us very much. Though we were spiritually dead because of the things we did against God, he gave us new life with Christ. You have been saved by God's grace.

Ephesians 2:4-5 NCV

more words of wisdom

God did everything necessary to provide for our forgiveness by sacrificing His perfect, holy Son as the atoning substitute for our sins.

Franklin Graham

**We cannot be right with God
until we are right with one another.**

Charles Swindoll

Jesus has affected human society like no other. The incomparable Christ is the good news. And what makes it such good news is that man is so undeserving but that God is so gracious.

John MacArthur

To be righteous means to be in right standing with God because your sins have been taken care of!

Kay Arthur

-A Tip-

You cannot do anything that God can't forgive. Accept His forgiveness today.

promises for life

God's Promises About...
HIS GUIDANCE

LORD, You light my lamp; my God illuminates my darkness.

Psalm 18:28 HCSB

The true children of God are those who let God's Spirit lead them.

Romans 8:14 NCV

The Lord says, "I will make you wise and show you where to go. I will guide you and watch over you."

Psalm 32:8 NCV

**In all your ways acknowledge Him,
and He shall direct your paths.**

Proverbs 3:6 NKJV

Every morning he wakes me. He teaches me to listen like a student. The Lord God helps me learn . . . .

Isaiah 50:4-5 NCV

EXTREME

more words of wisdom

Walk in the daylight of God's will because then you will be safe; you will not stumble.

Anne Graham Lotz

**If we want to hear God's voice,
we must surrender our minds and hearts to Him.**

Billy Graham

We have ample evidence that the Lord is able to guide. The promises cover every imaginable situation. All we need to do is to take the hand he stretches out.

Elisabeth Elliot

God will prove to you how good and acceptable and perfect His will is when He's got His hands on the steering wheel of your life.

Stuart & Jill Briscoe

-A Tip-

Pray for guidance. When you seek it, He will give it.

God's Promises About...
HIS LOVE

For the LORD your God has arrived to live among you. He is a mighty savior. He will rejoice over you with great gladness. With his love, he will calm all your fears. He will exult over you by singing a happy song.

Zephaniah 3:17 NLT

Unfailing love surrounds those who trust the LORD.

Psalm 32:10 NLT

But the love of the LORD remains forever with those who fear him. His salvation extends to the children's children of those who are faithful to his covenant, of those who obey his commandments!

Psalm 103:17-18 NLT

But God demonstrates His own love toward us, in that while we were still sinners, Christ died for us.

Romans 5:8 NKJV

For he chose us in him before the creation of the world to be holy and blameless in his sight. In love he predestined us to be adopted as his sons through Jesus Christ, in accordance with his pleasure and will . . . .

Ephesians 1:4-5 NIV

more words of wisdom

Even when we cannot see the why and wherefore of God's dealings, we know that there is love in and behind them, so we can rejoice always.

J. I. Packer

Being loved by Him whose opinion matters most gives us the security to risk loving, too—even loving ourselves.

Gloria Gaither

**There is no pit so deep
that God's love is not deeper still.**

Corrie ten Boom

Our hearts have been made to cry out for a love that can come only from our Creator.

Angela Thomas

-A Tip-

God's love makes everything look a lot better: When you invite the love of God into your heart, everything in the world looks different, including you.

GOd's Promises About...
HIS MERCY

For the LORD your God is a merciful God . . . .

Deuteronomy 4:31 NIV

If we claim that we're free of sin, we're only fooling ourselves. A claim like that is errant nonsense. On the other hand, if we admit our sins—make a clean breast of them—he won't let us down; he'll be true to himself. He'll forgive our sins and purge us of all wrongdoing.

1 John 1:8-9 MSG

All the prophets say it is true that all who believe in Jesus will be forgiven of their sins through Jesus' name.

Acts 10:43 NCV

But because of his great love for us, God, who is rich in mercy, made us alive with Christ even when we were dead in transgressions—it is by grace you have been saved.

Ephesians 2:4-5 NIV

But the mercy of the LORD is from everlasting to everlasting upon them that fear him, and his righteousness unto children's children . . . .

Psalm 103:17 KJV

more words of wisdom

Because his mercies are new every morning, you can find the courage to bring all of who you are to all of who he is.

Sheila Walsh

For God is, indeed, a wonderful Father who longs to pour out His mercy upon us, and whose majesty is so great that He can transform us from deep within.

St. Teresa of Avila

Jesus draws near to those who are afflicted and persecuted and criticized and ostracized.

Anne Graham Lotz

Mercy is an attribute of God, an infinite and inexhaustible energy within the divine nature which disposes God to be actively compassionate.

A. W. Tozer

-A Tip-

Because God is merciful to you, you can be merciful to others.

GOd's Promises About...
HIS PLAN

People may make plans in their minds, but the Lord decides what they will do.

Proverbs 16:9 NCV

"I say this because I know what I am planning for you," says the Lord. "I have good plans for you, not plans to hurt you. I will give you hope and a good future."

Jeremiah 29:11 NCV

It is God who works in you to will and to act according to his good purpose.

Philippians 2:13 NIV

There is no wisdom, no insight, no plan that can succeed against the LORD.

Proverbs 21:30 NIV

Unless the LORD builds a house, the work of the builders is useless.

Psalm 127:1 NLT

more words of wisdom

The one supreme business of life is to find God's plan for your life and live it.

E. Stanley Jones

**It's incredible to realize
that what we do each day has meaning
in the big picture of God's plan.**

Bill Hybels

God has a plan for the life of every Christian. Every circumstance, every turn of destiny, all things work together for your good and for His glory.

Billy Graham

With God, it's never "Plan B" or "second best." It's always "Plan A." And, if we let Him, He'll make something beautiful of our lives.

Gloria Gaither

-A Tip-

Big, bigger, and very big plans. God has very big plans in store for your life, so trust Him and wait patiently for those plans to unfold. And remember: God's timing is best.

promises for life

God's Promises About...
HIS PRESENCE

You will seek Me and find Me when you search for Me with all your heart.

Jeremiah 29:13 HCSB

Come near to God, and God will come near to you. You sinners, clean sin out of your lives. You who are trying to follow God and the world at the same time, make your thinking pure.

James 4:8 NCV

No, I will not abandon you as orphans—I will come to you.

John 14:18 NLT

The LORD is near all who call out to Him, all who call out to Him with integrity. He fulfills the desires of those who fear Him; He hears their cry for help and saves them.

Psalm 145:18-19 HCSB

Surely goodness and mercy shall follow me all the days of my life: and I will dwell in the house of the LORD for ever.

Psalm 23:6 KJV

more words of wisdom

There is nothing more important in any life than the constantly enjoyed presence of the Lord. There is nothing more vital, for without it we shall make mistakes, and without it we shall be defeated.

Alan Redpath

Through the death and broken body of Jesus Christ on the Cross, you and I have been given access to the presence of God when we approach Him by faith in prayer.

Anne Graham Lotz

God's presence is such a cleansing fire, confession and repentance are always there.

Anne Ortlund

The love of God is so vast, the power of his touch so invigorating, we could just stay in his presence for hours, soaking up his glory, basking in his blessings.

Debra Evans

-A Tip-

Having trouble hearing God? If so, slow yourself down, tune out the distractions, and listen carefully. God has important things to say; your task is to be still and listen.

promises for life

God's Promises About...
HIS PROTECTION

The LORD your God in your midst, The Mighty One, will save; He will rejoice over you with gladness, He will quiet you with His love, He will rejoice over you with singing.

Zephaniah 3:17 NKJV

Finally, my brethren, be strong in the Lord and in the power of His might. Put on the whole armor of God, that you may be able to stand against the wiles of the devil.

Ephesians 6:10-11 NKJV

I know whom I have believed and am persuaded that He is able to guard what has been entrusted to me until that day.

2 Timothy 1:12 HCSB

God is my shield, saving those whose hearts are true and right.

Psalm 7:10 NLT

Those who trust the Lord are like Mount Zion, which sits unmoved forever. As the mountains surround Jerusalem, the Lord surrounds his people now and forever.

Psalm 125:1-2 NCV

EXTREME

more words of wisdom

God will never let you sink under your circumstances. He always provides a safety net and His love always encircles.

Barbara Johnson

Only believe, don't fear. Our Master, Jesus, always watches over us, and no matter what the persecution, Jesus will surely overcome it.

Lottie Moon

Worries carry responsibilities that belong to God, not to you. Worry does not enable us to escape evil; it makes us unfit to cope with it when it comes.

Corrie ten Boom

A God wise enough to create me
and the world I live in is wise enough
to watch out for me.

Philip Yancey

-A Tip-

When you are in the center of God's will, you are in the center of God's protection.

God's Promises About...
HIS TIMING

To everything there is a season, a time for every purpose under heaven.

Ecclesiastes 3:1 NKJV

**He told them,
"You don't get to know the time.
Timing is the Father's business."**

Acts 1:7 MSG

Wait for the LORD; be strong and take heart and wait for the LORD.

Psalm 27:14 NIV

This is what the LORD says: "In the time of my favor I will answer you, and in the day of salvation I will help you . . . ."

Isaiah 49:8 NIV

Humble yourselves, therefore, under God's mighty hand, that he may lift you up in due time.

1 Peter 5:6 NIV

EXTREME

more words of wisdom

Even Jesus, clear as he was about his calling, had to get his instructions one day at a time. One time he was told to wait, another time to go.

Laurie Beth Jones

God does not promise to keep us out of the storms and floods, but He does promise to sustain us in the storm, and then bring us out in due time for His glory when the storm has done its work.

Warren Wiersbe

**God has a designated time
when his promise will be fulfilled
and the prayer will be answered.**

Jim Cymbala

-A Tip-

God has very big plans in store for your life, so trust Him and wait patiently for those plans to unfold. And remember: God's timing is best, so don't allow yourself to become discouraged if things don't work out exactly as you wish. Instead of worrying about your future, entrust it to God. He knows exactly what you need and exactly when you need it.

God's Promises About...
HOLY SPIRIT

When they were together for the last time they asked, "Master, are you going to restore the kingdom to Israel now? Is this the time?" He told them, "You don't get to know the time. Timing is the Father's business. What you'll get is the Holy Spirit. And when the Holy Spirit comes on you, you will be able to be my witnesses in Jerusalem, all over Judea and Samaria, even to the ends of the world."

Acts 1:6-9 MSG

There are diversities of gifts, but the same Spirit.

1 Corinthians 12:4 NKJV

And when they had prayed, the place was shaken where they were assembled together; and they were all filled with the Holy Ghost, and they spake the word of God with boldness.

Acts 4:31 KJV

But when the Holy Spirit controls our lives, he will produce this kind of fruit in us: love, joy, peace, patience, kindness, goodness, faithfulness, gentleness, and self-control. Here there is no conflict with the law.

Galatians 5:22-23 NLT

more words of wisdom

Whether we preach, pray, write, do business, travel, take care of children, or administer the government—whatever we do—our whole life and influence should be filled with the power of the Holy Spirit.

Charles Finney

The Holy Spirit is the divine substitute on earth today for the bodily presence of the Lord Jesus Christ two thousand years ago.

Alan Redpath

As I have continued to grow in my Christian maturity, I have discovered that the Holy Spirit does not let me get by with anything.

Anne Graham Lotz

The Lord Jesus by His Holy Spirit is with me, and the knowledge of His presence dispels the darkness and allays any fears.

Bill Bright

-A Tip-

The Holy Spirit is God in us, providing us with all we need to be effective Christians.

promises for life

God's Promises About...
HOPE

Let us hold on to the confession of our hope without wavering, for He who promised is faithful.

Hebrews 10:23 HCSB

The lines of purpose in your lives never grow slack, tightly tied as they are to your future in heaven, kept taut by hope.

Colossians 1:5 MSG

Now faith is the substance of things hoped for, the evidence of things not seen.

Hebrews 11:1 KJV

For I hope in You, O Lord; You will answer, O Lord my God.

Psalm 38:15 NASB

**The Lord is good to those whose hope is in him,
to the one who seeks him;
it is good to wait quietly
for the salvation of the Lord.**

Lamentations 3:25-26 NIV

more words of wisdom

Hope is faith holding out its hand in the dark.

Barbara Johnson

God's Word never said we were not to grieve our losses. It says we are not to grieve as those who have no hope (1 Thessalonians 4:13). Big Difference.

Beth Moore

Troubles we bear trustfully can bring us a fresh vision of God and a new outlook on life, an outlook of peace and hope.

Billy Graham

I discovered that sorrow was not to be feared but rather endured with hope and expectancy that God would use it to visit and bless my life.

Jill Briscoe

-A Tip-

Don't give up hope: Other people have experienced the same kind of hard times you may be experiencing now. They made it, and so can you. (Psalm 146:5)

God's Promises About...
HUMILITY

Therefore humble yourselves under the mighty hand of God, that He may exalt you at the proper time, casting all your anxiety on Him, because He cares for you.

1 Peter 5:6-7 NASB

You will save the humble people; But Your eyes are on the haughty, that You may bring them down.

2 Samuel 22:28 NKJV

Before honor is humility.

Proverbs 18:12 KJV

If My people who are called by My name will humble themselves, and pray and seek My face, and turn from their wicked ways, then I will hear from heaven, and will forgive their sin and heal their land.

2 Chronicles 7:14 NKJV

God has chosen you and made you his holy people. He loves you. So always do these things: Show mercy to others, be kind, humble, gentle, and patient.

Colossians 3:12 NCV

more words of wisdom

Seeking after God is a two-pronged endeavor. It requires not only humility to say, "God, I need you," but also a heart that desires a pure life that is pleasing to the Lord.

Jim Cymbala

If you know who you are in Christ, your personal ego is not an issue.

Beth Moore

That's what I love about serving God. In His eyes, there are no little people . . . because there are no big people. We are all on the same playing field. We all start at square one. No one has it better than the other, or possesses unfair advantage.

Joni Eareckson Tada

The gate of heaven is very low; only the humble can enter it.

Elizabeth Ann Seton

-A Tip-

Humility leads to happiness . . . pride doesn't. Max Lucado writes, "God exalts humility. When God works in our lives, helping us to become humble, he gives us a permanent joy. Humility gives us a joy that cannot be taken away." Enough said.

God's Promises About...
INTEGRITY

May integrity and uprightness protect me, because my hope is in you.

Psalm 25:21 NIV

Till I die, I will not deny my integrity. I will maintain my righteousness and never let go of it; my conscience will not reproach me as long as I live.

Job 27:5-6 NIV

People with integrity have firm footing,
but those who follow crooked paths
will slip and fall.

Proverbs 10:9 NLT

In everything set them an example by doing what is good. In your teaching show integrity, seriousness and soundness of speech that cannot be condemned, so that those who oppose you may be ashamed because they have nothing bad to say about us.

Titus 2:7 NIV

A good name is to be chosen rather than great riches, loving favor rather than silver and gold.

Proverbs 22:1 NKJV

more words of wisdom

God never called us to naïveté. He called us to integrity.... The biblical concept of integrity emphasizes mature innocence not childlike ignorance.

Beth Moore

Maintaining your integrity in a world of sham is no small accomplishment.

Wayne Oates

If you want to be proactive in the way you live your life, if you want to influence your life's direction, if you want your life to exhibit the qualities you find desireable, and if you want to live with integrity, then you need to know what your values are, decide to embrace them, and practice them every day.

John Maxwell

-A Tip-

One of your greatest possessions is integrity . . . don't lose it. Billy Graham was right when he said: "Integrity is the glue that holds our way of life together. We must constantly strive to keep our integrity intact. When wealth is lost, nothing is lost; when health is lost, something is lost; when character is lost, all is lost."

promises for life

God's Promises About...
JESUS

In the beginning was the Word, and the Word was with God, and the Word was God . . . . And the Word was made flesh, and dwelt among us, (and we beheld his glory, the glory as of the only begotten of the Father,) full of grace and truth.

John 1:1,14 KJV

At the name of Jesus every knee should bow, of those in heaven, and of those on earth, and of those under the earth, and that every tongue should confess that Jesus Christ is Lord, to the glory of God the Father.

Philippians 2:10-11 NKJV

For Jesus doesn't change— yesterday, today, tomorrow, he's always totally himself.

Hebrews 13:8 MSG

Let us run with endurance the race that is set before us, fixing our eyes on Jesus, the author and perfecter of faith, who for the joy set before Him endured the cross, despising the shame, and has sat down at the right hand of the throne of God.

Hebrews 12:1-2 NASB

more words of wisdom

Had Jesus been the Word become word, He would have spun theories about life, but since he was the Word become flesh, he put shoes on all his theories and made them walk.

E. Stanley Jones

Jesus be mine forever, my God, my heaven, my all.

C. H. Spurgeon

Abide in Jesus, the sinless one—which means, give up all of self and its life, and dwell in God's will and rest in His strength. This is what brings the power that does not commit sin.

Andrew Murray

**When we are in a situation where
Jesus is all we have,
we soon discover he is all we really need.**

Gigi Graham Tchividjian

-A Tip-

What a friend you have in Jesus: Jesus loves you, and He offers you eternal life with Him in heaven. Welcome Him into your heart. Now!

God's Promises About...
JOY

These things I have spoken to you, that My joy may remain in you, and that your joy may be full.

John 15:11 NKJV

Rejoice, and be exceeding glad: for great is your reward in heaven . . . .

Matthew 5:12 KJV

Thou wilt show me the path of life: in thy presence is fulness of joy; at thy right hand there are pleasures for evermore.

Psalm 16:11 KJV

A joyful heart is good medicine, but a broken spirit dries up the bones.

Proverbs 17:22 NASB

Always be full of joy in the Lord. I say it again—rejoice!

Philippians 4:4 NLT

EXTREME

more words of wisdom

Every morning is a fresh opportunity to find God's extraordinary joy in the most ordinary places.

Janet. L. Weaver

Finding joy means first of all finding Jesus.

Jill Briscoe

The Christian lifestyle is not one of legalistic do's and don'ts, but one that is positive, attractive, and joyful.

Vonette Bright

It is the definition of joy to be able to offer back to God the essence of what he's placed in you, be that creativity or a love of ideas or a compassionate heart or the gift of hospitality.

Paula Rinehart

True happiness and contentment cannot come from the things of this world. The blessedness of true joy is a free gift that comes only from our Lord and Savior, Jesus Christ.

Dennis Swanberg

-A Tip-

Joy does not depend upon your circumstances, but upon your relationship with God.

promises for life

God's Promises About...
LISTENING TO HIM

God has no use for the prayers of the people who won't listen to him.

Proverbs 28:9 MSG

The one who is from God listens to God's words. This is why you don't listen, because you are not from God.

John 8:47 HCSB

Listen in silence before me . . . .

Isaiah 41:1 NLT

Trust God from the bottom of your heart; don't try to figure out everything on your own. Listen for God's voice in everything you do, everywhere you go; he's the one who will keep you on track.

Proverbs 3:5-6 MSG

You must follow the LORD your God and fear Him. You must keep His commands and listen to His voice; you must worship Him and remain faithful to Him.

Deuteronomy 13:4 HCSB

more words of wisdom

When we come to Jesus stripped of pretensions, with a needy spirit, ready to listen, He meets us at the point of need.

Catherine Marshall

In the soul-searching of our lives, we are to stay quiet so we can hear Him say all that He wants to say to us in our hearts.

Charles Swindoll

**In prayer, the ear is of first importance.
It is of equal importance with the tongue,
but the ear must be named first.
We must listen to God.**

S. D. Gordon

An essential condition of listening to God is that the mind should not be distracted by thoughts of resentment, ill-temper, hatred or vengeance, all of which are comprised in the general term, the wrath of man.

R. V. G. Tasker

-A Tip-

Whether you are communicating with God or with others, try to listen more than talk.

promises for life

God's Promises About...
LOSS

He heals the brokenhearted and bandages their wounds.

Psalm 147:3 NCV

When I sit in darkness, the LORD will be a light to me.

Micah 7:8 NKJV

So those who suffer according to God's will should, in doing good, entrust themselves to a faithful Creator.

1 Peter 4:19 HCSB

I assure you: You will weep and wail, but the world will rejoice. You will become sorrowful, but your sorrow will turn to joy.

John 16:20 HCSB

***I have heard your prayer;
I have seen your tears.
Look, I will heal you.***

2 Kings 20:5 HCSB

EXTREME

more words of wisdom

When all else is gone, God is still left. Nothing changes Him.

Hannah Whitall Smith

Do not measure your loss by itself; if you do, it will seem intolerable; but if you will take all human affairs into account you will find that some comfort is to be derived from them.

St. Basil

As we focus on His love and Word, in time He will fill our void and loneliness, and He will heal our pain.

Anita Corrine Donihue

Loneliness is the first thing which God's eye named as not good.

John Milton

***When you feel that all is lost,
sometimes the greatest gain is ready to be yours.***

Thomas à Kempis

-A Tip-

When you realize that everything belongs to God, it eases the pain of loss.

God's Promises About...
LOVE

If I speak the languages of men and of angels, but do not have love, I am a sounding gong or a clanging cymbal.

1 Corinthians 13:1 HCSB

I pray that you, being rooted and firmly established in love, may be able to comprehend with all the saints what is the breadth and width, height and depth, and to know the Messiah's love that surpasses knowledge, so you may be filled with all the fullness of God.

Ephesians 3:17-19 HCSB

Above all, love each other deeply, because love covers over a multitude of sins.

1 Peter 4:8 NIV

**Now these three remain: faith, hope, and love.
But the greatest of these is love.**

1 Corinthians 13:13 HCSB

Dear friends, if God loved us in this way, we also must love one another.

1 John 4:11 HCSB

EXTREME

more words of wisdom

Life minus love equals zero.

George Sweeting

If Jesus is the preeminent One in our lives, then we will love each other, submit to each other, and treat one another fairly in the Lord.

Warren Wiersbe

Those who abandon ship the first time it enters a storm miss the calm beyond. And the rougher the storms weathered together, the deeper and stronger real love grows.

Ruth Bell Graham

**Love is an attribute of God.
To love others is evidence of a genuine faith.**

Kay Arthur

-A Tip-

Love at first sight always deserves a second look: If you give your heart away too easily or too often, you may find that it is returned to you . . . in very poor condition!

God's Promises About...
MIRACLES

Is anything impossible for the Lord?

Genesis 18:14 HCSB

For nothing will be impossible with God.

Luke 1:37 HCSB

You are the God who works wonders; You revealed Your strength among the peoples.

Psalm 77:14 HCSB

I assure you: The one who believes in Me will also do the works that I do. And he will do even greater works than these, because I am going to the Father.

John 14:12 HCSB

Looking at them, Jesus said, "With men it is impossible, but not with God, because all things are possible with God."

Mark 10:27 HCSB

more words of wisdom

I could go through this day oblivious to the miracles all around me or I could tune in and "enjoy."

Gloria Gaither

Are you looking for a miracle? If you keep your eyes wide open and trust in God, you won't have to look very far.

Marie T. Freeman

To be a Christian is to believe in the impossible. Jesus was God. Jesus was human.

Madeleine L'Engle

The most profane word we use is "hopeless." When you say a situation or person is hopeless, you are slamming the door in the face of God.

Kathy Troccoli

**Only God can move mountains,
but faith and prayer can move God.**

E. M. Bounds

-A Tip-

If you're looking for miracles . . . you'll find them. If you're not, you won't.

God's Promises About...
MISTAKES

Flee from youthful passions, and pursue righteousness, faith, love, and peace, along with those who call on the Lord from a pure heart.

2 Timothy 2:22 HCSB

If we confess our sins to him, he is faithful and just to forgive us and to cleanse us from every wrong.

1 John 1:9 NLT

Have mercy on me, O God, according to your unfailing love; according to your great compassion blot out my transgressions. Wash away all my iniquity and cleanse me from my sin.

Psalm 51:1-2 NIV

Instead, God has chosen the world's foolish things to shame the wise, and God has chosen the world's weak things to shame the strong.

1 Corinthians 1:27 HCSB

A man's own foolishness leads him astray, yet his heart rages against the LORD.

Proverbs 19:3 HCSB

more words of wisdom

We become a failure when we allow mistakes to take away our ability to learn, give, grow, and try again.

Susan Lenzkes

There is nothing wrong with asking God's direction. But it is wrong to go our own way, then expect Him to bail us out.

Larry Burkett

Father, take our mistakes and turn them into opportunities.

Max Lucado

Mistakes offer the possibility for redemption and a new start in God's kingdom. No matter what you're guilty of, God can restore your innocence.

Barbara Johnson

Lord, when we are wrong, make us willing to change; and when we are right, make us easy to live with.

Peter Marshall

-A Tip-

Made a mistake? Ask for forgiveness! If you've broken one of God's rules, you can always ask Him for His forgiveness. And He will always give it!

promises for life

God's Promises About...
MODERATION

An overseer, then, must be above reproach, the husband of one wife, temperate, prudent, respectable, hospitable, able to teach, not addicted to wine or pugnacious, but gentle, peaceable, free from the love of money.

1 Timothy 3:2-3 NASB

**For what will it profit a man
if he gains the whole world,
and loses his own soul?
Or what will a man give
in exchange for his soul?**

Mark 8:36-37 NKJV

I discipline my body and make it my slave.

1 Corinthians 9:27 NASB

No one can serve two masters; for either he will hate the one and love the other, or he will be devoted to one and despise the other. You cannot serve God and wealth.

Matthew 6:24 NASB

EXTREME

more words of wisdom

We are all created differently. We share a common need to balance the different parts of our lives.

Dr. Walt Larimore

When I feel like circumstances are spiraling downward in my life, God taught me that whether I'm right side up or upside down, I need to turn those circumstances over to Him. He is the only one who can bring balance into my life.

Carole Lewis

Every moment of resistance to temptation is a victory.

Frederick William Faber

To many, total abstinence is easier than perfect moderation.

St. Augustine

Contentment has a way of quieting insatiable desires.

Mary Hunt

-A Tip-

Adopt healthy habits that you can stick with. In other words, don't starve yourself. Be moderate, even in your moderation.

God's Promises About...
OBEDIENCE

I have sought You with all my heart; don't let me wander from Your commands.

Psalm 119:10 HCSB

It is the LORD your God you must follow, and him you must revere. Keep his commands and obey him; serve him and hold fast to him.

Deuteronomy 13:4 NIV

**The world and its desires pass away,
but the man who does
the will of God lives forever.**

1 John 2:17 NIV

Just then someone came up and asked Him, "Teacher, what good must I do to have eternal life?" "Why do you ask Me about what is good?" He said to him. "There is only One who is good. If you want to enter into life, keep the commandments."

Matthew 19:16-17 HCSB

EXTREME

more words of wisdom

When you suffer and lose, that does not mean you are being disobedient to God. In fact, it might mean you're right in the center of His will. The path of obedience is often marked by times of suffering and loss.

Charles Swindoll

The strength and happiness of a man consists in finding out the way in which God is going, and going that way too.

Henry Ward Beecher

Mary could not have dreamed all that would result from her faithful obedience. Likewise, you cannot possibly imagine all that God has in store for you when you trust him.

Henry Blackaby

**Obedience goes before our hearts
and carries them
where they would not normally go.**

Paula Rinehart

-A Tip-

Obey God or face the consequences: God rewards obedience and punishes disobedience. It's not enough to understand God's rules; you must also live by them . . . or else.

promises for life

God's Promises About...
OPPORTUNITIES

Make the most of every opportunity.

Colossians 4:5 NIV

Remember ye not the former things, neither consider the things of old. Behold, I will do a new thing . . . .

Isaiah 43:18-19 KJV

I can do everything through him that gives me strength.

Philippians 4:13 NIV

Let us not lose heart in doing good, for in due time we shall reap if we do not grow weary. So then, while we have opportunity, let us do good to all men, and especially to those who are of the household of the faith.

Galatians 6:9-10 NASB

Dear brothers and sisters, whenever trouble comes your way, let it be an opportunity for joy. For when your faith is tested, your endurance has a chance to grow. So let it grow, for when your endurance is fully developed, you will be strong in character and ready for anything.

James 1:2-4 NLT

more words of wisdom

Every day we live is a priceless gift of God, loaded with possibilities to learn something new, to gain fresh insights.

Dale Evans Rogers

A wise man makes more opportunities than he finds.

Francis Bacon

**God surrounds you with opportunity.
You and I are free in Jesus Christ,
not to do whatever we want,
but to be all that God wants us to be.**

Warren Wiersbe

-A Tip-

Familiarize yourself with the opportunities of tomorrow: The world of tomorrow is filled with opportunities for those who are willing to find them and work for them. Make certain that you have more than a passing familiarity with ever shifting sands of our changing America. Then, share your insights with the young people around you.

God's Promises About...
OPTIMISM

Make me to hear joy and gladness . . . .

Psalm 51:8 KJV

For God has not given us a spirit of fearfulness, but one of power, love, and sound judgment.

2 Timothy 1:7 HCSB

But we are hoping for something we do not have yet, and we are waiting for it patiently.

Romans 8:25 NCV

**My cup runs over.
Surely goodness and mercy shall follow me
all the days of my life; and I will dwell
in the house of the LORD forever.**

Psalm 23:5-6 NKJV

Be of good courage, and he shall strengthen your heart, all ye that hope in the LORD.

Psalm 31:24 KJV

EXTREME

more words of wisdom

The people whom I have seen succeed best in life have always been cheerful and hopeful people who went about their business with a smile on their faces.

Charles Kingsley

If you can't tell whether your glass is half-empty or half-full, you don't need another glass; what you need is better eyesight . . . and a more thankful heart.

Marie T. Freeman

Stop thinking wishfully and start living hopefully.

Emilie Barnes

The game was to just find something about everything to be glad about—no matter what it was. You see, when you're hunting for the glad things, you sort of forget the other kind.

Eleanor H. Porter

-A Tip-

Be a realistic optimist: Your attitude toward the future will help create your future. You might as well put the self-fulfilling prophecy to work for you, and besides, life is far too short to be a pessimist.

God's Promises About...
PATIENCE

Patience is better than strength.

Proverbs 16:32 ICB

We urge you, brethren, admonish the unruly, encourage the fainthearted, help the weak, be patient with everyone.

1 Thessalonians 5:14 NASB

Be completely humble and gentle; be patient, bearing with one another in love.

Ephesians 4:2 NIV

Patience and encouragement come from God. And I pray that God will help you all agree with each other the way Christ Jesus wants.

Romans 15:5 NCV

But if we look forward to something we don't have yet, we must wait patiently and confidently.

Romans 8:25 NLT

EXTREME

more words of wisdom

Waiting means going about our assigned tasks, confident that God will provide the meaning and the conclusions.

Eugene Peterson

Waiting is the hardest kind of work, but God knows best, and we may joyfully leave all in His hands.

Lottie Moon

**God is more patient with us
than we are with ourselves.**

Max Lucado

Let me encourage you to continue to wait with faith. God may not perform a miracle, but He is trustworthy to touch you and make you whole where there used to be a hole.

Lisa Whelchel

-A Tip-

Henry Blackaby writes, "The grass that is here today and gone tomorrow does not require much time to mature. A big oak tree that lasts for generations requires much more time to grow and mature. God is concerned about your life through eternity. Allow Him to take all the time He needs to shape you for His purposes. Larger assignments will require longer periods of preparation." How true!

God's Promises About...
PEACE

God has called us to peace.

1 Corinthians 7:15 NKJV

I leave you peace; my peace I give you. I do not give it to you as the world does. So don't let your hearts be troubled or afraid.

John 14:27 NCV

If it is possible, as far as it depends on you, live at peace with everyone.

Romans 12:18 NIV

Live peaceful and quiet lives in all godliness and holiness.

1 Timothy 2:2 NIV

***You, Lord, give true peace
to those who depend on you,
because they trust you.***

Isaiah 26:3 NCV

EXTREME

more words of wisdom

I want first of all . . . to be at peace with myself. I want a singleness of eye, a purity of intention, a central core to my life . . . . I want, in fact—to borrow from the language of the saints—to live "in grace" as much of the time as possible.

Anne Morrow Lindbergh

Prayer guards hearts and minds and causes God to bring peace out of chaos.

Beth Moore

**When we do what is right,
we have contentment, peace, and happiness.**

Beverly LaHaye

The Christian has a deep, silent, hidden peace, which the world sees not, like some well in a retired and shady place.

John Henry Cardinal Newman

-A Tip-

God's peace can be yours right now. . . if you open up your heart and invite Him in.

God's Promises About...
PERSEVERANCE

For you need endurance, so that after you have done God's will, you may receive what was promised.

Hebrews 10:36 HCSB

Let us not become weary in doing good, for at the proper time we will reap a harvest if we do not give up.

Galatians 6:9 NIV

**It is better to finish something than to start it.
It is better to be patient than to be proud.**

Ecclesiastes 7:8 NCV

Pursue righteousness, godliness, faith, love, endurance, and gentleness. Fight the good fight for the faith; take hold of eternal life, to which you were called and have made a good confession before many witnesses.

1 Timothy 6:11-12 HCSB

EXTREME

more words of wisdom

In all negotiations of difficulties, a man may not look to sow and reap at once. He must prepare his business and so ripen it by degrees.

Francis Bacon

Just remember, every flower that ever bloomed had to go through a whole lot of dirt to get there!

Barbara Johnson

Battles are won in the trenches, in the grit and grime of courageous determination; they are won day by day in the arena of life.

Charles Swindoll

Don't give up. Moses was once a basket case!

Anonymous

-A Tip-

The world encourages instant gratification but God's work takes time. Remember the words of C. H. Spurgeon: "By perseverance, the snail reached the ark."

God's Promises About...
PLEASING HIM

I tried keeping rules and working my head off to please God, and it didn't work. So I quit being a "law man" so that I could be God's man. Christ's life showed me how, and enabled me to do it. I identified myself completely with him. Indeed, I have been crucified with Christ. My ego is no longer central.

Galatians 2:19-20 MSG

He said to them, "You make yourselves look good in front of people, but God knows what is really in your hearts. What is important to people is hateful in God's sight."

Luke 16:15 NCV

Everything that goes into a life of pleasing God has been miraculously given to us by getting to know, personally and intimately, the One who invited us to God. The best invitation we ever received!

2 Peter 1:3 MSG

**Our only goal is to please God
whether we live here or there,
because we must all stand before
Christ to be judged.**

2 Corinthians 5:9-10 NCV

EXTREME

more words of wisdom

If you really want to please God and intend to be in full agreement with His will, you can't go wrong.

Francis Mary Paul Libermann

You will get untold flak for prioritizing God's revealed and present will for your life over man's . . . but, boy, is it worth it.

Beth Moore

You must never sacrifice your relationship with God for the sake of a relationship with another person.

Charles Stanley

It is impossible to please God doing things motivated by and produced by the flesh.

Bill Bright

-A Tip-

Pleasing other people is important sometimes. But pleasing God is important all of the time.

God's Promises About...
PRAISE

I will praise You with my whole heart.

Psalm 138:1 NKJV

And suddenly there was with the angel a multitude of the heavenly host praising God and saying: "Glory to God in the highest, And on earth peace, goodwill toward men!"

Luke 2:13-14 NKJV

In everything give thanks;
for this is the will of God in Christ Jesus for you.

2 Thessalonians 5:18 NKJV

Is anyone happy? Let him sing songs of praise.

James 5:13 NIV

Through Him then, let us continually offer up a sacrifice of praise to God, that is, the fruit of lips that give thanks to His name.

Hebrews 13:15 NASB

EXTREME

more words of wisdom

The time for universal praise is sure to come some day. Let us begin to do our part now.

Hannah Whitall Smith

Praise reestablishes the proper chain of command; we recognize that the King is on the throne and that he has saved his people.

Max Lucado

Nothing we do is more powerful or more life-changing than praising God.

Stormie Omartian

Maintaining a focus on God will take our praise to heights that nothing else can.

Jeff Walling

-A Tip-

Praise Him! One of the main reasons you go to church is to praise God. But, you need not wait until Sunday rolls around to thank your Heavenly Father. Instead, you can praise Him many times each day by saying silent prayers that only He can hear.

God's Promises About...
PRAYER

And everything—whatever you ask in prayer, believing—you will receive.

Matthew 21:22 HCSB

The intense prayer of the righteous is very powerful.

James 5:16 HCSB

**Rejoice in hope; be patient in affliction;
be persistent in prayer.**

Romans 12:12 HCSB

Rejoice always! Pray constantly. Give thanks in everything, for this is God's will for you in Christ Jesus.

1 Thessalonians 5:16-18 HCSB

Therefore I want the men in every place to pray, lifting up holy hands without anger or argument.

1 Timothy 2:8 HCSB

EXTREME

more words of wisdom

Prayer isn't just preparation for the battle; prayer is the battle.

Bob Logan

It is well said that neglected prayer is the birth-place of all evil.

C. H. Spurgeon

Obedience is the master key to effective prayer.

Billy Graham

Prayer guards hearts and minds and causes God to bring peace out of chaos.

Beth Moore

Cultivating a heart of prayer is a sure way to experience God's presence.

Elizabeth George

-A Tip-

Pray early and often: One way to make sure that your heart is in tune with God is to pray often. The more you talk to God, the more He will talk to you.

God's Promises About...
PRIORITIES

**First pay attention to me, and then relax.
Now you can take it easy—
you're in good hands.**

Proverbs 1:33 MSG

And I pray this: that your love will keep on growing in knowledge and every kind of discernment, so that you can determine what really matters and can be pure and blameless in the day of Christ.

Philippians 1:9 HCSB

He said to them all, "If anyone desires to come after Me, let him deny himself, and take up his cross daily, and follow Me. For whoever desires to save his life will lose it, but whoever loses his life for My sake will save it."

Luke 9:23-24 NKJV

Let us fix our eyes on Jesus, the author and perfecter of our faith, who for the joy set before him endured the cross, scorning its shame, and sat down at the right hand of the throne of God.

Hebrews 12:2 NIV

EXTREME

more words of wisdom

How important it is for us—young and old—to live as if Jesus would return any day—to set our goals, make our choices, raise our children, and conduct business with the perspective of the imminent return of our Lord.

Gloria Gaither

Great relief and satisfaction can come from seeking God's priorities for us in each season, discerning what is "best" in the midst of many noble opportunities, and pouring our most excellent energies into those things.

Beth Moore

Sin is largely a matter of mistaken priorities. Any sin in us that is cherished, hidden, and not confessed will cut the nerve center of our faith.

Catherine Marshall

**No horse gets anywhere until he is harnessed.
No life ever grows great
until it is focused, dedicated, disciplined.**

Harry Emerson Fosdick

-A Tip-

Unless you put first things first, you're bound to finish last: And don't forget that putting first things first means God first.

promises for life

GOd's Promises About...
PROBLEMS

For when the way is rough, your patience has a chance to grow. So let it grow, and don't try to squirm out of your problems.

James 1:3-4 TLB

People who do what is right may have many problems, but the Lord will solve them all.

Psalm 34:19 NCV

When you go through deep waters and great trouble, I will be with you. When you go through the rivers of difficulty, you will not drown! When you walk through the fire of oppression, you will not be burned up; the flames will not consume you. For I am the LORD, your God . . . .

Isaiah 43:2-3 NLT

Come to me, all you who are weary and burdened, and I will give you rest. Take my yoke upon you and learn from me, for I am gentle and humble in heart, and you will find rest for your souls. For my yoke is easy and my burden is light.

Matthew 11:28-30 NIV

EXTREME

more words of wisdom

Don't duck the most difficult problems. That just insures that the hardest part will be left when you're most tired. Get the big one done, and it's all downhill from then on.

Norman Vincent Peale

What a comfort to know that God is present there in your life, available to meet every situation with you, that you are never left to face any problem alone.

Vonette Bright

**Always remember that problems
contain values that have improvement potential.**

Norman Vincent Peale

Don't let controversy hurt your soul. Live near to God by prayer. Just fall down at His feet and open your very soul before Him, and throw yourself right into His arms.

Catherine Booth

-A Tip-

When it comes to solving problems, work beats worry. Remember: It is better to fix than to fret.

GOd's Promises About...
PURPOSE

We know that all things work together for the good of those who love God: those who are called according to His purpose.

Romans 8:28 HCSB

Whatever you do, do all to the glory of God.

1 Corinthians 10:31 NKJV

You're sons of Light, daughters of Day. We live under wide open skies and know where we stand. So let's not sleepwalk through life . . . .

1 Thessalonians 5:5-6 MSG

I will instruct you and show you the way to go; with My eye on you, I will give counsel.

Psalm 32:8 HCSB

You reveal the path of life to me; in Your presence is abundant joy; in Your right hand are eternal pleasures.

Psalm 16:11 HCSB

EXTREME

more words of wisdom

Aim at Heaven and you will get earth "thrown in"; aim at earth and you will get neither.

C. S. Lewis

God custom-designed you with your unique combination of personality, temperament, talents, and background, and He wants to harness and use these in His mission to reach this messed-up world.

Bill Hybels

We aren't just thrown on this earth like dice tossed across a table. We are lovingly placed here for a purpose.

Charles Swindoll

Finding one's mission, and then fulfilling it, is perhaps the most vital activity in which a person can engage.

Laurie Beth Jones

-A Tip-

God still has a wonderful plan for your life. And the time to start looking for that plan—and living it—is now.

GOd's Promises About...
QUIET TIME

Be still, and know that I am God.

Psalm 46:10 NKJV

In quietness and trust is your strength.

Isaiah 30:15 NASB

Be silent before the LORD
and wait expectantly for Him.

Psalm 37:7 HCSB

I wait quietly before God, for my hope is in him.

Psalm 62:5 NLT

What's this? Fools out shopping for wisdom! They wouldn't recognize it if they saw it!

Proverbs 17:16 MSG

EXTREME

more words of wisdom

The manifold rewards of a serious, consistent prayer life demonstrate clearly that time with our Lord should be our first priority.

Shirley Dobson

When we are in the presence of God, removed from distractions, we are able to hear him more clearly, and a secure environment has been established for the young and broken places in our hearts to surface.

John Eldredge

The Lord Jesus, available to people much of the time, left them, sometimes a great while before day, to go up to the hills where He could commune in solitude with His Father.

Elisabeth Elliot

Most of man's trouble comes from his inability to be still.

Blaise Pascal

-A Tip-

Begin each day with a few minutes of quiet time to organize your thoughts. During this time, read at least one uplifting Bible passage and thus begin your day on a positive, productive note.

promises for life

God's Promises About...
RENEWAL

Create in me a pure heart, O God, and renew a steadfast spirit within me. Do not cast me from your presence or take your Holy Spirit from me. Restore to me the joy of your salvation and grant me a willing spirit, to sustain me.

Psalm 51:10-12 NIV

**The One who was sitting on the throne said,
"Look! I am making everything new!"
Then he said, "Write this, because these words
are true and can be trusted."**

Revelation 21:5 NCV

But may the God of all grace, who called us to His eternal glory by Christ Jesus, after you have suffered a while, perfect, establish, strengthen, and settle you.

1 Peter 5:10 NKJV

He makes me to lie down in green pastures; He leads me beside the still waters. He restores my soul; He leads me in the paths of righteousness For His name's sake.

Psalm 23:2-3 NKJV

EXTREME

more words of wisdom

In those desperate times when we feel like we don't have an ounce of strength, He will gently pick up our heads so that our eyes can behold something—something that will keep His hope alive in us.

Kathy Troccoli

He is the God of wholeness and restoration.

Stormie Omartian

God gives us permission to forget our past and the understanding to live our present. He said He will remember our sins no more. (Psalm 103:11-12)

Serita Ann Jakes

Walking with God leads to receiving his intimate counsel, and counseling leads to deep restoration.

John Eldredge

-A Tip-

God is in the business of making all things new: Vance Havner correctly observed, "God is not running an antique shop! He is making all things new!" And that includes you.

God's Promises About...
REPENTANCE

When you are in distress and all these things have happened to you, you will return to the LORD your God in later days and obey Him. He will not leave you, destroy you, or forget the covenant with your fathers that He swore to them by oath, because the LORD your God is a compassionate God.

Deuteronomy 4:30-31 HCSB

I preached that they should repent and turn to God and prove their repentance by their deeds.

Acts 26:20 NIV

Come back to the LORD and live!

Amos 5:6 NLT

There will be more joy in heaven over one sinner who repents than over 99 righteous people who don't need repentance.

Luke 15:7 HCSB

But the Pharisees and their scribes were complaining to His disciples, "Why do you eat and drink with tax collectors and sinners?" Jesus replied to them, "The healthy don't need a doctor, but the sick do. I have not come to call the righteous, but sinners to repentance."

Luke 5:30-32 HCSB

more words of wisdom

Repentance was perhaps best defined by a small girl: It's to be sorry enough to quit.

C. H. Kilmer

Sorrow for sin is as indispensable as faith.

C. H. Spurgeon

When true repentance comes, God will not hesitate for a moment to forgive, cast the sins in the sea of forgetfulness, and put the child on the road to restoration.

Beth Moore

Repentance begins with confession of our guilt and recognition that our sin is against God.

Charles Stanley

In repentance, we must be truly sorry for our sin, and we must express our intent to turn away from it.

Shirley Dobson

-A Tip-

First, confess your sins to God. Then, ask Him what actions you should take in order to make things right again.

promises for life

God's Promises About...
RESURRECTION

Now on the first day of the week, very early in the morning, they, and certain other women with them, came to the tomb bringing the spices which they had prepared. But they found the stone rolled away from the tomb. Then they went in and did not find the body of the Lord Jesus. And it happened, as they were greatly perplexed about this, that behold, two men stood by them in shining garments. Then, as they were afraid and bowed their faces to the earth, they said to them, "Why do you seek the living among the dead? He is not here, but is risen!"

Luke 24:1-6 NKJV

For I passed on to you as most important what I also received: that Christ died for our sins according to the Scriptures, that He was buried, that He was raised on the third day according to the Scriptures.

1 Corinthians 15:3-4 HCSB

For I know that my Redeemer lives.

Job 19:25 NKJV

EXTREME

more words of wisdom

The resurrection of Jesus Christ is the power of God to change history and to change lives.

Bill Bright

The stone was rolled away from the tomb not so Jesus could get out, but so that the world could look in. His resurrection assures yours. Because He lives, you will live forever.

Charles Stanley

The Resurrection is the biggest news in history. CNN ought to put it on Headline News every thirty minutes. It should scream from every headline: Jesus is alive!

Dennis Swanberg

The resurrection of Jesus, the whole alphabet of human hope, the certificate of our Lord's mission from heaven, is the heart of the gospel in all ages.

R. G. Lee

-A Tip-

The resurrection was real, and Jesus is alive! That's the difference between Christianity and all other religions.

promises for life

God's Promises About...
RIGHTEOUSNESS

Because the eyes of the Lord are on the righteous and His ears are open to their request. But the face of the Lord is against those who do evil.

1 Peter 3:12 HCSB

Walk in a manner worthy of the God who calls you into His own kingdom and glory.

1 Thessalonians 2:12 NASB

Discipline yourself for the purpose of godliness.

1 Timothy 4:7 NASB

Therefore, come out from among them and be separate, says the Lord; do not touch any unclean thing, and I will welcome you.

2 Corinthians 6:17 HCSB

Flee from youthful passions, and pursue righteousness, faith, love, and peace, along with those who call on the Lord from a pure heart.

2 Timothy 2:22 HCSB

EXTREME

more words of wisdom

We are in desperate need for women of faith who are willing to courageously stand against sin and stand for righteousness.

Susan Hunt

Righteousness not only defines God, but God defines righteousness.

Bill Hybels

There is but one good; that is God. Everything else is good when it looks to Him and bad when it turns from Him.

C. S. Lewis

Have your heart right with Christ, and he will visit you often, and so turn weekdays into Sundays, meals into sacraments, homes into temples, and earth into heaven.

C. H. Spurgeon

Sanctify yourself and you will sanctify society.

St. Francis of Assisi

-A Tip-

Avoid people and places that might tempt you to disobey God's commandments.

promises for life

God's Promises About...
SEEKING HIM

It is impossible to please God apart from faith. And why? Because anyone who wants to approach God must believe both that he exists and that he cares enough to respond to those who seek him.

Hebrews 11:6 MSG

**You will seek me and find me
when you seek me with all your heart.**

Jeremiah 29:13 NIV

Draw near to God, and He will draw near to you.

James 4:8 HCSB

The Lord is good to those whose hope is in him, to the one who seeks him.

Lamentations 3:25 NIV

Let the hearts of those who seek the Lord rejoice. Look to the Lord and his strength; seek his face always.

1 Chronicles 16:10-11 NIV

EXTREME

more words of wisdom

To approach God requires neither art nor science, but only a heart resolutely determined to apply itself to nothing but Him, or for His sake, and to love Him only.

Brother Lawrence

Thirsty hearts are those whose longings have been wakened by the touch of God within them.

A. W. Tozer

We rarely discover anything monumental about God without discovering something momentous about ourselves. With every revelation comes an invitation to adjust our lives to what we have seen.

Beth Moore

Whenever you seek truth, you seek God, whether or not you know it.

Edith Stein

-A Tip-

Nobody can find Him for you. God is searching for you; it's up to you—and you alone—to open your heart to Him.

promises for life

God's Promises About...
SIN

For all have sinned and fall short of the glory of God.

Romans 3:23 HCSB

If we say that we have no sin, we deceive ourselves, and the truth is not in us. If we confess our sins, He is faithful and just to forgive us our sins and to cleanse us from all unrighteousness.

1 John 1:8-9 NKJV

All who indulge in a sinful life are dangerously lawless, for sin is a major disruption of God's order.

1 John 3:4 MSG

It is written: There is no one righteous, not even one.

Romans 3:10 HCSB

The one who conceals his sins will not prosper, but whoever confesses and renounces them will find mercy.

Proverbs 28:13 HCSB

EXTREME

more words of wisdom

Sin will take you farther than you'll want to go; sin will leave you longer than you'll want to stay; sin will cost you far more than you'll want to pay.

Quips, Anonymous

If you want to be saved, quit your sinful ways. You need not be skipping around the Lord with the devil's old musket on your shoulder.

Sam Jones

God is so compassionate and ready to forgive! He sees our heart and knows when we have humbled ourselves in repentance. Then, he immediately forgives. It doesn't matter how terrible the sin; he is looking for a repentant heart that he can forgive.

Mary Morrison Suggs

-A Tip-

Confess your sin as soon as you recognize it. God will forgive you, and then you can forgive yourself.

promises for life

God's Promises About...
SPIRITUAL GROWTH

Run away from infantile indulgence. Run after mature righteousness—faith, love, peace—joining those who are in honest and serious prayer before God.

2 Timothy 2:22 MSG

For this reason we also, since the day we heard it, do not cease to pray for you, and to ask that you may be filled with the knowledge of His will in all wisdom and spiritual understanding.

Colossians 1:9 NKJV

So let us stop going over the basics of Christianity again and again. Let us go on instead and become mature in our understanding.

Hebrews 6:1 NLT

Know the love of Christ which surpasses knowledge, that you may be filled up to all the fullness of God.

Ephesians 3:19 NASB

EXTREME

more words of wisdom

Don't go through life, grow through life.

Eric Butterworth

God does not discipline us to subdue us, but to condition us for a life of usefulness and blessedness.

Billy Graham

Each moment of our existence, we are either growing into more or retreating into less.

Brennan Manning

We have tasted "that the Lord is good" (Psalm 34:8), but we don't yet know how good he is. We only know that his sweetness makes us long for more.

C. H. Spurgeon

Growing in any area of the Christian life takes time, and the key is daily sitting at the feet of Jesus.

Cynthia Heald

-A Tip-

Spiritual maturity is a journey, not a destination.

God's Promises About...
STRENGTH

Be of good courage, and let us be strong for our people and for the cities of our God. And may the LORD do what is good in His sight.

1 Chronicles 19:13 NKJV

**You, therefore, my child,
be strong in the grace that is in Christ Jesus.**

2 Timothy 2:1 HCSB

Do you not know? Have you not heard? The Everlasting God, the LORD, the Creator of the ends of the earth does not become weary or tired. His understanding is inscrutable. He gives strength to the weary, and to him who lacks might He increases power. Though youths grow weary and tired, and vigorous young men stumble badly, yet those who wait for the LORD will gain new strength; they will mount up with wings like eagles, they will run and not get tired, they will walk and not become weary.

Isaiah 40:28-31 NASB

He said unto me, My grace is sufficient for thee: for my strength is made perfect in weakness.

2 Corinthians 12:9 KJV

more words of wisdom

God conquers only what we yield to Him. Yet, when He does, and when our surrender is complete, He fills us with a new strength that we could never have known by ourselves. His conquest is our victory!

Shirley Dobson

God is the One who provides our strength, not only to cope with the demands of the day, but also to rise above them. May we look to Him for the strength to soar.

Jim Gallery

God gives us always strength enough, and sense enough, for everything he wants us to do.

John Ruskin

**The greatness of man's power
is the measure of his surrender.**

William Booth

-A Tip-

Need strength? Let God's Spirit reign over your heart. Anne Graham Lotz writes, "The amount of power you experience to live a victorious, triumphant Christian life is directly proportional to the freedom you give the Spirit to be Lord of your life!" And remember that the best time to begin living triumphantly is the present moment.

promises for life

God's Promises About...
SUCCESS

The one who acquires good sense loves himself; one who safeguards understanding finds success.

Proverbs 19:8 HCSB

Let us not become weary in doing good, for at the proper time we will reap a harvest if we do not give up.

Galatians 6:9 NIV

But as for you, be strong and do not give up, for your work will be rewarded.

2 Chronicles 15:7 NIV

The one who understands a matter finds success, and the one who trusts in the LORD will be happy.

Proverbs 16:20 HCSB

Remember this: the person who sows sparingly will also reap sparingly, and the person who sows generously will also reap generously.

2 Corinthians 9:6 HCSB

more words of wisdom

Nothing in this world is more fundamental for success in life than hope, and this star pointed to our only source of true hope: Jesus Christ.

D. James Kennedy

There's not much you can't achieve or endure if you know God is walking by your side. Just remember: Someone knows, and Someone cares.

Bill Hybels

We, as believers, must allow God to define success. And, when we do, God blesses us with His love and His grace.

Jim Gallery

Success or failure can be pretty well predicted by the degree to which the heart is fully in it.

John Eldredge

God's never been guilty of sponsoring a flop.

Ethel Waters

-A Tip-

Don't let others define success for you. That's between you and God.

promises for life

God's Promises About...
TALENTS

According to the grace given to us, we have different gifts: If prophecy, use it according to the standard of faith; if service, in service; if teaching, in teaching; if exhorting, in exhortation; giving, with generosity; leading, with diligence; showing mercy, with cheerfulness.

Romans 12:6-8 HCSB

Do not neglect the gift that is in you.

1 Timothy 4:14 HCSB

Each one has his own gift from God, one in this manner and another in that.

1 Corinthians 7:7 NKJV

His master said to him, "Well done, good and faithful slave! You were faithful over a few things; I will put you in charge of many things. Enter your master's joy!"

Matthew 25:21 HCSB

Every good gift and every perfect gift is from above, and cometh down from the Father of lights.

James 1:17 KJV

more words of wisdom

If you want to reach your potential, you need to add a strong work ethic to your talent.

John Maxwell

You are the only person on earth who can use your ability.

Zig Ziglar

Your heavenly Father created you with unique gifts and untapped talents; your job is to tap them sooner rather than never.

Criswell Freeman

Not everyone possesses boundless energy or a conspicuous talent. We are not equally blessed with great intellect or physical beauty or emotional strength. But we have all been given the same ability to be faithful.

Gigi Graham Tchividjian

-A Tip-

Each person possesses special abilities that can be nurtured carefully or ignored totally. The challenge, of course, is to do the former and to avoid the latter.

promises for life

God's Promises About...
THANKSGIVING

Thanks be to God for His indescribable gift!

2 Corinthians 9:15 NKJV

Our prayers for you are always spilling over into thanksgivings. We can't quit thanking God our Father and Jesus our Messiah for you!

Colossians 1:3 MSG

Finally, brethren, whatsoever things are true, whatsoever things are honest, whatsoever things are just, whatsoever things are pure, whatsoever things are lovely, whatsoever things are of good report; if there be any virtue, and if there be any praise, think on these things.

Philippians 4:8 KJV

Make a joyful noise unto the Lord all ye lands. Serve the LORD with gladness: come before his presence with singing. Know ye that the LORD he is God: it is he that hath made us, and not we ourselves; we are his people and the sheep of his pasture. Enter into his gates with thanksgiving, and into his courts with praise; be thankful unto him and bless his name. For the LORD is good; his mercy is everlasting; and his truth endureth to all generations.

Psalm 100 KJV

EXTREME

more words of wisdom

God is in control, and therefore in everything I can give thanks, not because of the situation, but because of the One who directs and rules over it.

Kay Arthur

Thanksgiving is good but Thanksliving is better.

Jim Gallery

Thanksgiving or complaining—these words express two contrastive attitudes of the souls of God's children in regard to His dealings with them. The soul that gives thanks can find comfort in everything; the soul that complains can find comfort in nothing.

Hannah Whitall Smith

Thanksgiving invites God to bestow a second benefit.

Robert Herrick

-A Tip-

Don't overlook God's gifts: Every sunrise represents yet another beautifully wrapped gift from God. Unwrap it, treasure it, use it, and give thanks to the Giver.

promises for life

God's Promises About...
THE FEAR OF GOD

Don't consider yourself to be wise; fear the LORD and turn away from evil.

Proverbs 3:7 HCSB

**Honor all people. Love the brotherhood.
Fear God. Honor the king.**

1 Peter 2:17 NKJV

Brothers, sons of Abraham's race, and those among you who fear God, the message of this salvation has been sent to us.

Acts 13:26 HCSB

The fear of the LORD is the beginning of wisdom, and the knowledge of the Holy One is understanding.

Proverbs 9:10 HCSB

You must follow the LORD your God and fear Him. You must keep His commands and listen to His voice; you must worship Him and remain faithful to Him.

Deuteronomy 13:4 HCSB

EXTREME

more words of wisdom

It is an act of the will to allow God to be our refuge. Otherwise, we live outside of his love and protection, wondering why we feel alone and afraid.

Mary Morrison Suggs

A healthy fear of God will do much to deter us from sin.

Charles Swindoll

The remarkable thing about fearing God is that when you fear God, you fear nothing else, whereas if you do not fear God, you fear everything else.

Oswald Chambers

It is not possible that mortal men should be thoroughly conscious of the divine presence without being filled with awe.

C. H. Spurgeon

It is only the fear of God that can deliver us from the fear of man.

John Witherspoon

-A Tip-

It's the right kind of fear . . . Your respect for God should make you fearful of disobeying Him . . . very fearful.

God's Promises About...
THOUGHTS

Those who are pure in their thinking are happy, because they will be with God.

Matthew 5:8 NCV

**So prepare your minds for service
and have self-control.**

1 Peter 1:13 NCV

Come near to God, and God will come near to you. You sinners, clean sin out of your lives. You who are trying to follow God and the world at the same time, make your thinking pure.

James 4:8 NCV

And now, dear brothers and sisters, let me say one more thing as I close this letter. Fix your thoughts on what is true and honorable and right. Think about things that are pure and lovely and admirable. Think about things that are excellent and worthy of praise.

Philippians 4:8 NLT

Dear friend, guard Clear Thinking and Common Sense with your life; don't for a minute lose sight of them. They'll keep your soul alive and well, they'll keep you fit and attractive.

Proverbs 3:21-22 MSG

more words of wisdom

The mind is like a clock that is constantly running down. It has to be wound up daily with good thoughts.

Fulton J. Sheen

As we have by faith said no to sin, so we should by faith say yes to God and set our minds on things above, where Christ is seated in the heavenlies.

Vonette Bright

No more imperfect thoughts. No more sad memories. No more ignorance. My redeemed body will have a redeemed mind. Grant me a foretaste of that perfect mind as you mirror your thoughts in me today.

Joni Eareckson Tada

**Attitude is the mind's paintbrush;
it can color any situation.**

Barbara Johnson

-A Tip-

Watch what you think: If your inner voice is, in reality, your inner critic, you need to tone down the criticism now. And while you're at it, train yourself to begin thinking thoughts that are more rational, more accepting, and less judgmental.

promises for life

God's Promises About...
TRUSTING HIM

And God, in his mighty power, will protect you until you receive this salvation, because you are trusting him.

1 Peter 1:5 NLT

Those who trust in the LORD are as secure as Mount Zion; they will not be defeated but will endure forever.

Psalm 125:1 NLT

The Good News shows how God makes people right with himself—that it begins and ends with faith. As the Scripture says, "But those who are right with God will live by trusting in him."

Romans 1:17 NCV

Do not let your hearts be troubled. Trust in God; trust also in me. In my Father's house are many rooms; if it were not so, I would have told you. I am going there to prepare a place for you.

John 14:1-2 NIV

EXTREME

more words of wisdom

You will trust God only as much as you love him. And you will love him not because you have studied him; you will love him because you have touched him—in response to his touch.

Brennan Manning

God delights to meet the faith of one who looks up to Him and says, "Lord, You know that I cannot do this—but I believe that You can!"

Amy Carmichael

It helps to resign as the controller of your fate. All that energy we expend to keep things running right is not what keeps things running right.

Anne Lamott

**Never be afraid to trust
an unknown future to a known God.**

Corrie ten Boom

-A Tip-

It's simple: depend upon God: Remember the words of Vance Havner: "We must live in all kinds of days, both high days and low days, in simple dependence upon Christ as the branch on the vine. This is the supreme experience."

promises for life

God's Promises About...
TRUTH

Be diligent to present yourself approved to God, a worker who doesn't need to be ashamed, correctly teaching the word of truth.

2 Timothy 2:15 HCSB

Therefore laying aside falsehood, speak truth, each one of you, with his neighbor, for we are members of one another.

Ephesians 4:25 NASB

Jesus answered, "I am the way and the truth and the life. No one comes to the Father except through me."

John 14:6 NIV

**I have no greater joy than this:
to hear that my children are walking in the truth.**

3 John 1:4 HCSB

You have already heard about this hope in the message of truth, the gospel that has come to you. It is bearing fruit and growing all over the world, just as it has among you since the day you heard it and recognized God's grace in the truth.

Colossians 1:5-6 HCSB

EXTREME

more words of wisdom

The difficult truth about truth is that it often requires us to change our perspectives, attitudes, and rules for living.

Susan Lenzkes

The only people who achieve much are those who want knowledge so badly that they seek it while the conditions are still unfavorable. Favorable conditions never come.

C. S. Lewis

For Christians, God himself is the only absolute; truth and ethics are rooted in his character.

Chuck Colson

To worship Him in truth means to worship Him honestly, without hypocrisy, standing open and transparent before Him.

Anne Graham Lotz

-A Tip-

Watch what you say and what you don't say: Remember: some of the most hurtful falsehoods are told in silence.

God's Promises About...
WISDOM

Therefore, everyone who hears these words of Mine and acts on them will be like a sensible man who built his house on the rock. The rain fell, the rivers rose, and the winds blew and pounded that house. Yet it didn't collapse, because its foundation was on the rock.

Matthew 7:24-25 HCSB

The Lord says, "I will make you wise and show you where to go. I will guide you and watch over you."

Psalm 32:8 NCV

**Wisdom is the principal thing;
therefore get wisdom.
And in all your getting, get understanding.**

Proverbs 4:7 NKJV

But from Him you are in Christ Jesus, who for us became wisdom from God, as well as righteousness, sanctification, and redemption.

1 Corinthians 1:30 HCSB

For God has not given us a spirit of fearfulness, but one of power, love, and sound judgment.

2 Timothy 1:7 HCSB

more words of wisdom

Indeed, wisdom and discernment are among the natural results of a prayer-filled life.

Richard Foster

Don't expect wisdom to come into your life like great chunks of rock on a conveyor belt. Wisdom comes privately from God as a byproduct of right decisions, godly reactions, and the application of spiritual principles to daily circumstances.

Charles Swindoll

Knowledge is horizontal.
Wisdom is vertical; it comes down from above.

Billy Graham

Wisdom always waits for the right time to act, while emotion always pushes for action right now.

Joyce Meyer

-A Tip-

Don't be satisfied with the acquisition of knowledge . . . strive to acquire wisdom. As Beth Moore correctly observed, "A big difference exists between a head full of knowledge and the words of God literally abiding in us."

GOd's Promises About...
WORK

But one thing I do: Forgetting what is behind and straining toward what is ahead, I press on toward the goal to win the prize for which God has called me heavenward in Christ Jesus.

Philippians 3:13-14 NIV

**In all the work you are doing,
work the best you can.
Work as if you were doing it for the Lord,
not for people.**

Colossians 3:23 NCV

Be strong and brave, and do the work. Don't be afraid or discouraged, because the Lord God, my God, is with you. He will not fail you or leave you.

1 Chronicles 28:20 NCV

Then He said to His disciples, "The harvest truly is plentiful, but the laborers are few."

Matthew 9:37 NKJV

The people had a mind to work.

Nehemiah 4:6 KJV

more words of wisdom

God's strategy is silence, then action—waiting or resting, then work. Have you noticed it?

Anne Ortlund

We must trust as if it all depended on God and work as if it all depended on us.

C. H. Spurgeon

Thank God every morning when you get up that you have something which must be done, whether you like it or not. Work breeds a hundred virtues that idleness never knows.

Charles Kingsley

It may be that the day of judgment will dawn tomorrow; in that case, we shall gladly stop working for a better tomorrow. But not before.

Dietrich Bonhoeffer

Faith and work make a triumphant combination.

Father Flanagan

-A Tip-

Goofing off is contagious. That's why it's important for you to hang out with people who are interested in getting the job done right—and getting it done right now!